Praise for *Breaking Failure*

"As a 15-year marketing professional responsible for many campaign and product launches, reading *Breaking Failure* helped bring into focus my own planning and post-campaign assessment shortcomings. The author does an excellent job introducing a framework as well as techniques any manager can use to better identify, gauge, quantify and most importantly lessen the impact of failure. Detailed infographics and examples help the reader understand the power and applicability of each of these techniques. The author also does a good job illustrating how these techniques can be incorporated across any organization. *Breaking Failure* is a must read for any manager looking to improve business performance and avoid recurring pitfalls."

—**Andrew Franco**, Vice President of Marketing at Transamerica

"In *Breaking Failure*, Alexander Edsel breathes new life into an age-old question: Can businesses prevent and mitigate failure? The short answer is yes, but the strength of Edsel's approach is the way in which he convincingly transfers the insights of fields such as engineering into the marketing arena while also demonstrating their practical use and implementation potential. Edsel presents an intuitive suite of frameworks that address management biases, identify and prioritize risks, establish mechanisms for warnings, and develop strategies to prevent and prepare for failure. Highly recommended for the marketing practitioner who is looking for an actionable, pragmatic approach to dealing with failure, an inevitable reality of doing business."

—**Yannis Kotziagkiaouridis**, Global Chief Analytics Officer at Wunderman

"Author Alexander Edsel has created a rich story that removes the mystery surrounding product success and failure, offering a refreshing blend of street wisdom and classical theory to apply problem-solving techniques from other disciplines into the crazy world of marketing and product management."

—**Jeff Kavanaugh**, VP and Managing Partner, Infosys Consulting

"With all the buzz in marketing today around big data and technology as the way to improve our craft, Alexander Edsel reminds us that the best opportunities for progress may come from looking outside of our discipline and applying decision-making principles from other domains. Since reading Edsel's book, I've changed the way I think about solving marketing problems and just as importantly have changed the way I think about staffing, giving much more weight to the need for cross-disciplinary thinking in our hiring."

—**Patricia Lyle**, General Manager, Meredith Xcelerated Marketing

"I've worked with Alex on a number of projects, and I appreciate his ability to communicate highly technical concepts to executable actions for real business professionals. This book isn't just for CEOs and senior executives; it's also for managers and employees looking to implement improvement processes to create real value in their businesses. As Alex points outs, the techniques do require a modest investment in time but most importantly the discipline to apply these practices on a consistent and concentrated basis to mitigate potential future failure."

—**Mike Hart**, Vice President of Sales, Lennox Industries, Inc.

"Alex brings perspective on the real-world challenges that are faced by businesses today. His approach to diagnosing issues early, applying past learnings, and hopefully ending up with better outcomes will help all enterprises from small to large improve their performance."

—**Bob Nolan**, Senior Vice President of Insights & Analytics, ConAgra Foods

"By identifying key areas where corporate failures typically originate from, Alexander Edsel lays out a roadmap for decision-makers to listen, assess, understand, and strategize to avoid or minimize the impact of catastrophic failures. This is an excellent, practical treatise to effect a learning, evidence-based organization where tools, process, concept-testing and empowerment replace gut-feelings and unsubstantiated domain-transfer generalizations. An excellent resource that should help trigger deeper thinking."

—**Dimitris Tsioutsias**, Ph.D. / SVP, Strategic Business Analytics,
Targetbase-Omnicom Media Group

"At a time when everyone in business is talking about being data-driven, but very few enterprises are actually benefiting from it, *Breaking Failure* provides a much needed set of frameworks and methodologies to guide decision making and maximize the impact of business investments. Complex concepts are laid out clearly and can be followed easily, making them ultimately practical and applicable. And maybe most importantly, the book is relevant to multiple levels of managers and executives, as well as across organizational functions, from marketing to operations and HR."

—**Slavi Samardzija**, Chief Analytics Officer, Annalect-Omnicom Media Group

"Alexander Edsel's perspective in *Breaking Failure* is key for businesses to use effective problem solving tools normally used for process improvement. By using his methodology, businesses can focus on the true reasons for the occurrence and abate failures before they occur, saving time and money. A book to add to my 'Lean Library' collection."

—**Lisa Townsend**, Business Excellence Manager, Lennox Industries

Breaking Failure

Breaking Failure

How to Break the Cycle of Business Failure and Underperformance Using Root Cause, Failure Mode and Effects Analysis, and an Early Warning System

Alexander D. Edsel

Publisher: Paul Boger
Editor-in-Chief: Amy Neidlinger
Executive Editor: Jeanne Glasser Levine
Cover Designer: Chuti Prasertsith
Managing Editor: Kristy Hart
Project Editor: Andy Beaster
Copy Editor: Keith Cline
Proofreader: Language Logistics, Chrissy White
Indexer: Tim Wright
Senior Compositor: Gloria Schurick
Manufacturing Buyer: Dan Uhrig

Publishing as FT Press

Upper Saddle River, New Jersey 07458

For information about buying this title in bulk quantities, or for special sales opportunities (which may include electronic versions; custom cover designs; and content particular to your business, training goals, marketing focus, or branding interests), please contact our corporate sales department at corpsales@pearsoned.com or (800) 382-3419.

For government sales inquiries, please contact governmentsales@pearsoned.com.

For questions about sales outside the U.S., please contact international@pearsoned.com.

Printed in the United States of America

First Printing October 2015

ISBN-10: 0-13-438636-1
ISBN-13: 978-0-13-438636-2

Pearson Education LTD.
Pearson Education Australia PTY, Limited.
Pearson Education Singapore, Pte. Ltd.
Pearson Education Asia, Ltd.
Pearson Education Canada, Ltd.
Pearson Educación de Mexico, S.A. de C.V.
Pearson Education—Japan
Pearson Education Malaysia, Pte. Ltd.

Library of Congress Control Number: 2015946542

To my wife, Karen, and our wonderful children
Alex, James, Philip and Paul,
may you learn from failure and be
successful managing the most important
domain transfer the future holds.

To my departed parents, Ernest and Cristina,
for their unconditional love and guidance.

I especially want to dedicate this book
in memory of my father,
whom I credit with providing me
with the original concept for the book.

Contents

Acknowledgments

I want to thank many of my past and current colleagues and deans at the Jindal School of Management, the University of Texas at Dallas, and especially Professors Dr. B.P.S. Murthi and Abhijit Biswas, for their role in my hiring and support throughout my career at UT Dallas.

I also wish to acknowledge all my industry colleagues who over time and in different ways have contributed to my knowledge. I especially wish to acknowledge and thank Faith Chandler from NASA, Patricia Lyle, Slavi Samardzija, Randy Wahl, Bob Nolan, Babar Bhatti, Jeff Kavanaugh, Hal Brierley, and Rob High for their feedback or information that was incorporated into this book.

None of this would have been possible without the advice and help of my book agents, Maryann Karinch and Zachary Gajewski from the Rudy Agency, as well as the publication team at Pearson.

About the Author

Alexander D. Edsel is the Director of the Master of Science in Marketing program for the Naveen Jindal School of Business at the University of Texas at Dallas, where he has been a faculty member for more than 12 years. In addition, he has more than 20 years of product management and marketing management experience in both B2B and B2C markets in the chemical, high-tech, and healthcare fields while at Bayer, Compaq, and WellPoint. His original work and research on failure and underperformance began in 1996 and was first published in March 2011 with an article that appeared in the Product Development Management Association's *Vision* magazine. Edsel holds both MBA and JD degrees. In his spare time, he loves to read nonfiction books, spend time with his family, and explore additional failure-mitigation techniques at his blog at www.breakingfailure.com.

Introduction

"The obscure we see eventually. The completely obvious, it seems, takes longer."

—Edward R. Murrow, American broadcast journalist

When Harry Markowitz, winner of the 1990 Nobel Prize in Economics for his portfolio management theory, was asked how he allocated his investments, he replied, "I should have computed the historical covariances of the asset classes and drawn an efficient frontier... Instead, I split my contributions 50/50 between bonds and equities." Everyone has probably experienced this phenomenon whereby you analyze—maybe even use—sophisticated models to evaluate business challenges or opportunities but rarely apply the same amount of time, effort, or diligence to your personal finances or endeavors.

This paradoxical but common occurrence was described by Nassim Taleb, author of *The Black Swan: The Impact of the Highly Improbable,* as domain dependence or the inability to transfer a proven technique, process, or concept from one discipline or industry to another.

This book looks at why this blind spot occurs within different disciplines and professions. Identifying useful techniques from other domains and applying them to a different discipline is a simple yet transformational act that can yield a higher ROI than any of the incremental optimizations performed by companies. Also, it is not as if these domain transfers do not work; if challenged, everyone can think of highly beneficial knowledge or best practices adopted from other disciplines or industries. The origins of statistics, for example, began with the analysis of census data by governments many hundreds of years ago, evolving and improving over time. The adoption of statistics by other disciplines was accelerated by the development of probability theory first used by astronomers in the 19th century. Other disciplines soon followed, including business, which began using statistics in the early 20th century and which became the foundation for finance, operations management, and many areas in marketing. Another widely adopted domain transfer by business was the Stage-Gate system, which has become the de facto standard for new product development in many categories. The Stage-Gate concept originated with chemical engineering in the 1940s as a technique for developing new compounds. It was then adopted and refined by NASA in the 1960s for use in "phased project planning." Dr. Robert Cooper is credited with formalizing and refining this concept for new product development in business in his 1994 blockbuster book, *Winning at New Products*. According to Cooper, he arrived at the Stage-Gate concept by observing what successful companies like DuPont were doing in this field. It is no small coincidence that DuPont was in the chemical industry, where the technique originated.

Domain transfers should not be confused with applying a different framework, sometimes incorrectly, to another industry or situation, as occurred during the short tenure of JCPenney's CEO Ron Johnson. Johnson, the former Senior VP of Retail Operations at Apple, managed during his 16-month tenure at JCPenney to lose over a billion dollars in revenue and caused the company to suffer a 50 percent drop in its stock price. Johnson's sin was to default to his usual framework—the Apple way—where consumer market testing, sales, and discounts were never used. Johnson believed that the Apple framework would work just as well in the nontech retail world of apparel, shoes, furniture, kitchenware, and knick-knacks. Addressing framework mistakes and how they can be prevented is the subject of Chapter 2, "Don't Start Off on the Wrong Foot."

State of Management

It is especially important to apply these failure mitigation and prevention techniques that we will cover in this book to areas like advertising, human resources, marketing, sales, strategy, and product management because despite the fact they are considered more "science" and less "art," they still lack many of the standard protocols, continuing professional education requirements, and mandatory professional certifications found in other disciplines such as law, medicine, or accounting. Case in point: Even though the study of statistics is widely accepted by marketing and taught in most academic programs, it is used correctly and on a regular basis by probably fewer than 15 percent of marketing professionals. While there are some functional areas in marketing where statistics are less important (e.g., event management), there are still many areas where it should be used but isn't. Most lead generation campaigns, for example, do not usually conduct split A/B tests, which is a related problem: the partial adoption of a domain transfer. Moreover, most business professionals have no grasp of statistical traps such as when correlations do not have a cause-and-effect relationship.

The premise of this book can be boiled down to three observations. Most failures and underperformance are due to the following:

- Error-prone thinking and decision making
- Voids in the domain transfer of proven techniques that would be useful to many areas of business (e.g., failure mode and effects analysis, root cause analysis, and an early warning system)
- A deficient and inconsistent knowledge base among many business professionals due to the lack of mandatory professional certifications and continuing education (finance and especially accounting being two notable exceptions)

This book proposes solutions to address the first two problems, but the third requires the collaborative effort of agencies, Fortune 1000 companies, academia, and professional organizations.

Applicability of These Concepts

The techniques presented in this book can be used by any company regardless of size or industry type. However, some techniques when applied to large, complex organizations, such as the Failure Mode and Effects Analysis or Root Cause Analysis, will require a team effort and are somewhat process-intensive, requiring some time and effort, especially when conducted for the first time. The best way to determine when to use these domain transfers is to initially use them on your most expensive and mission-critical campaigns or product launches and then decide what the threshold should be to use or not use them. For some companies, it might be when more than $10,000 is at risk; for others, the threshold might be when more than $100,000 is at risk. Once a company becomes proficient with these techniques, the time and effort required should decrease considerably. Other techniques, such as the early warning system and preplanned exit strategy, require only a one-time effort with adjustments over time.

Benefiting from the Topic

"*Volume hides a multitude of sins*" is one of those wisdom-laden quotes of unknown origin but of profound significance to this book and topic. As explained in *Breaking Failure,* business failure and underperformance is more prevalent and likely to occur than most people suspect. However, all failures and underperformances are not equal. At large corporations, mistakes that would sink a small or medium-sized company are often swept under the rug or shrugged off. There is also the emotional and family sacrifice that business failure can bring to individuals in start-ups and smaller companies. While the book is of benefit to everyone, it is especially important to those with the most "skin in the game," be it in their careers or business.

The book is like a workout; it requires more focus than if reading a "get rich quick," theoretical or opinion type business book. However, as with a workout when done correctly, it can translate into very tangible benefits. In addition, expensive and complex solutions have been eliminated from this book so that any small, medium-sized, or large company can benefit from its easy-to-understand concepts and techniques. These techniques do require a relatively modest investment, but only in time and not money. The bigger challenge, similar to exercise, is in developing the discipline to apply these techniques on a regular basis.

Many of the case studies used are about launching and managing products or about conducting different types of campaigns. However, these techniques can be used in any area of business, such as Human Resources to determine why 30 percent of new hires underperform and have to be let go after 12 months (using a Root Cause Analysis). It can be used by the Strategy or Mergers and Acquisition group to analyze all the things that could go wrong with a new company acquisition (using a Failure Mode and Effects Analysis) or by the Finance department to see why their investment choices are underperforming. In this last example, contributors to failure may have included immediate causes such as a sudden increase in the interest rate. What this book explains is how to go beyond that and find out what faulty decisions or assumptions led to the undesired outcome.

Finally, the ROI and benefits from applying these techniques should be readily apparent given that they have been proven and used by other disciplines and industries for decades—just not in key areas in business such as innovation, strategy, marketing, product management, sales, and finance.

1

Failure & Stagnation

"Failure isn't fatal, but failure to change might be."

—John Wooden, the "Wizard of Westwood" (As head coach at UCLA, Wooden won ten NCAA national championships in a 12-year period.)

If a cruise ship carrying 1,000 passengers had a major emergency at sea (i.e., a failure) and the passengers had to evacuate the ship but at that critical moment learned that there were no preplanned evacuation guidelines, life jackets, or lifeboats, and that the crew had never trained for an evacuation, most people would consider this an act of criminal negligence. Although lives are not usually at risk in a business context, few companies have a preplanned contingency response, exit plan, or the necessary training in place to identify, mitigate, and handle failure when they launch a new business, product, or expensive marketing campaign. This omission is in great measure due to the lack of awareness about how high the probability of failure or underperformance actually is. Obviously, those odds are much higher than the likelihood of a cruise ship sinking.

Failure, Failure Everywhere

Usually, the media spend most of their time highlighting the amazing feats of a few individuals or companies, creating the illusion or perception that this type of success is more commonplace than it really is. If this illusion were balanced by the actual ratio of failure and underperformance to highly successful ventures, we might even see a dip in entrepreneurial activity. Moreover, the few failures reported are usually oversimplified and attributed to management, when in fact it is often due to a confluence of factors the media would be hard pressed to uncover, given their need for quick and simple storylines.

Business failures are thus like an iceberg with spectacular large company failures (e.g., Motorola's Iridium or BlackBerry post-iPhone), the visible tip floating above the surface. While it is common knowledge that a significant percentage of new products fail shortly after launch, less known is that many products fail at later stages in the product life cycle, or substantially underperform throughout their existence. These other factors are like the larger 90 percent mass of the iceberg hidden beneath the ocean waves.

How pervasive is product failure? It is difficult to provide a specific number applicable to all industries. For one thing, there aren't many new or definitive studies on the subject, and existing studies tend to be industry specific or based on surveys. Survey-based failure-rate studies tend to understate the incidence of failure due to "nonresponse" and interviewee bias. After all, most companies and managers who have experienced failure are inclined to either minimize the failure or avoid discussing it altogether. Another factor making it difficult to quantify failure is that its definition may vary in regards to both its time frame and monetary amount. For example, when a product is dropped after the fifth year, despite the projected life cycle being ten years, should that be considered a failure? Should a product that underperformed the forecasted rate of return by 20 percent but was never dropped be considered a failure?

Let's keep those challenges in mind while examining some of the data for outright failures. A survey by the *Product Development & Management Association* (PDMA) found that only one out of every ten product concepts becomes a commercial success, and new products have a failure rate of 42 percent.[1] The Conference Board reported a median failure rate of 34 percent for consumer products and 36 percent for industrial products.[2] A Booz Allen Hamilton study cited a 35 percent failure rate for new product launches.[3] An even gloomier assessment is from *New Product News*, a trade magazine, which found a new product failure rate of 80 percent.[4] Chicago consultant Kuczmarski & Associates analyzed the success rates of 1,000 new products launched by 77 manufacturing, service, and consumer products companies. They found only a little more than half (56 percent) of all products launched are still on the market five years later.[5] Figure 1.1 from the U.S. Bureau of Labor reveals how after five years, 50 percent of new businesses will have failed. By the fifteenth year, approximately 75 percent of original businesses will no longer be around.

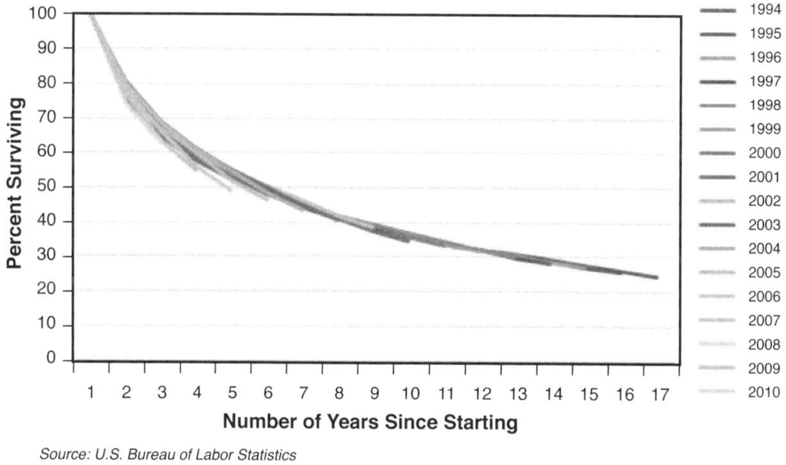

Figure 1.1 Survival rates of establishments, by year started and number of years since starting, 1994–2010

One industry-specific study by Linton Matysiak & Wilkes, a market research and new product development firm for the food industry, reviewed 1,935 new products to determine overall product, new item, and line extension mortality; line extension to new item ratios;

regional breakdowns; and national introductions.[6] The findings were as follows:

- The failure rate for new product introduction in the retail grocery industry was somewhere in the 70 to 80 percent range.
- The "top 20" food companies in the United States experienced a 24 percent failure rate for new product introductions, and the "bottom 20,000" U.S. food companies had an 88 percent failure rate for new product introductions.

Some authorities on new product introductions such as C.M. Crawford and James Cooper believe, as the LMW study suggests, that failure rates vary by company/industry and that the more marketing-savvy companies (i.e., Fortune 500 types) have failure rates more in the 15 percent range, whereas other companies might have failure rates in the 80 percent range, for an overall median failure rate of around 35 percent.[7] Nevertheless, many large companies with a long history in consumer marketing have experienced high failure rates. In the 1980s, for example, Campbell Soup Company launched approximately 160 new products a year worldwide, with a failure rate of 80 percent.[8] One factor that might also explain the lower rate of product failure in larger companies is their heavy reliance on line extensions. Although they tend to have a lower outright failure rate, they also often cannibalize sales and erode the positioning of the entire product line. Confirming this high ratio of product line extensions is a Booz Allen Hamilton report on the breakdown of new products by type, which reveals that approximately 40 percent of new product introductions are actually either additions or improvements to existing products.[9]

The major downside for these larger companies is that when they do experience failure or underperformance, their exposure tends to be of a magnitude many times larger than that of other companies. Procter & Gamble is such a company. Considered a pioneer in the marketing field, P&G has had its share of expensive flops, such as its fat-free but tasteless snack containing Olestra, which incurred a $250 million loss. Also consider Reflect.com, an online customizable cosmetic offering, which closed after six years in the market at a $60 million loss.[10]

Unfortunately, the failure rate of products and services has not declined in the past several decades, despite advances in information and data analytics. In fact, it is one of the few remaining areas whereby an improvement and reduction in the failure rate could easily double or triple a company's profitability. Table 1.1 lists the losses incurred by major business failures during the past 20 years, highlighting the greater magnitude of failure that many large companies experience, including some considered to be marketing savvy.

Table 1.1 Major Business and Product Failures

Product	Loss
Mercedes Benz's purchase of Chrysler	$30 billion
Tesco Fresh & Easy	$3 billion
Iridium	$2.5 billion
Snapple (under Quaker Oats)	$1.1 billion
Webvan	$1 billion
Hewlett-Packard's TouchPad	$885 million
Selecta Vision by RCA	$580 million
Texas Instruments TI99 PC	$500 million
Ford's Edsel	$400 million
Premier Smokeless by RJR	$325 million
Pets.com	$300 million
Amex Optima	$265 million
Zapmail by FedEx	$230 million
Nissan ad campaign "Enjoy the Ride," which resulted in declining sales	$200 million
IBM's PCjr (introduced in March 1985)	$100 million
Corfam by Dupont (synthetic leather)	$100 million
Polavision by Polaroid	$68 million
TV's CableWeek by Time Inc.	$47 million
Campbell's Fresh Thinking	$25 million

Underperformance

If one also considers all the products or campaigns that were not outright failures but that performed below their forecasted potential (with a rate of return below the standard for that industry or sector), the chances of failure or underperformance are disturbingly high. For example, Hewlett-Packard's smartphone product line (the iPaq inherited from the merger with Compaq) experienced meager growth during a five-year period and was finally dropped in 2011, although it could have been kept on life support even longer. Moreover, this mediocre performance occurred during a time when the smartphone industry was booming.[11]

One study on underperformance by Alvin Achenbaum using SAMI-Burke data found that of the dozens of thousands of products introduced in the past ten years, fewer than 200 had more than $15 million in annual sales, and only a handful produced more than $100 million.[12] A study by Copernicus Marketing (a subsidiary of the billion-dollar agency Aegis Dentsu) of more than 500 marketing programs revealed that 84 percent of those programs fail to have a positive return.[13] Nielsen suggested, in a recent report, a failure and underperformance rate for new products approaching 85 percent. In this same study, Nielsen looked at 3,463 launches in 2012, of which only 14 products met the criteria necessary for enduring and long-term success as measured by factors closely associated with blockbuster products such as their distinctiveness, relevance, and endurance.[14]

This underperformance issue can also be inferred from company performance data, such as a report by the Education Foundation of the National Federation of Independent Business, which estimated that over the lifetime of a business, 39 percent are profitable, 30 percent break even, and 30 percent lose money (with 1 percent falling in the "unable to determine" category).[15] By taking the 35 percent median outright failure rate and adding in 30 percent as an approximation for underperforming companies (e.g., stuck in a marginal returns or break-even mode), it can be said that the average failure and underperformance rate is in the 65 percent range, with lower rates for resource-abundant larger companies and higher rates for smaller companies.

The Overlooked Costs of Failure: The Intangibles and Opportunity Costs

While most failure calculations, if performed at all, only consider the financial cost of failure, many other factors are not usually considered, such as the damage to the brand and company's reputation, employee morale, management's time, vendor relationships, and, if a public company, investor confidence. The reason these consequences of failure are often left out from any monetary calculation is because they are often difficult to quantify. However, if these intangibles are not included in your calculations, the impact of failure will be significantly understated.

Another overlooked victim of failure are the opportunities not pursued as a result of launching the business, product, or campaign that ended in failure or underperformance. The time and money invested in the failed venture that could have gone into a more productive venture should also be factored in. This calculation can be as simple as the interest rate that would have accrued if the cash had been placed in a three- or five-year Treasury bill versus the failed initiative. An even better benchmark, if the market has abnormally low interest rates, is to estimate the projected revenue from a modest market share increase from targeting your existing products and current customers (i.e., increasing the volume/frequency of purchase) or the industry average rate of return for non-high-risk ventures.

If one were to attempt to quantify the cost of a failed product and included these additional factors, the results might look like the hypothetical shown in Table 1.2 of a failed launch for a medium-sized company.

Table 1.2 A More Holistic Calculation of Losses

1. Monetary losses: capital investments, salaries, unsellable inventory, advertising and promotional expenses, and so on.	2. Damage to brand (i.e., 20 percent loss in brand equity).	3. Management's time and reputation; damage to vendor-distributor relationship and employee morale.	4. Lost opportunity costs: 6 percent of the $3 million.	True cost of this failed product is approximately 20 percent higher than initially thought.
$3M	$200K	$300K	$180K	$3.68M

The Clogged Pipeline

Many new products often don't make it to the launch or commercialization stage, which may not seem to be a problem; it all depends on how expensive and time-consuming it is to get a product to these final stages. If you are a pharmaceutical company, it matters a great deal. If you are a restaurant trying to come up with new menu items, it is not as problematic. A high ratio of potential new products entering the development pipeline but not making it to launch could indicate a problem with the initial screening stages. The bigger problem occurs when too many ideas are reaching the testing stage (usually Stage IV) but not going on to commercialization, which is significant given that this stage is the most time-consuming and expensive. These are examples of clogging up the development pipeline.

Every company should establish a benchmark or threshold as to how many products that make it to the final stages should launch successfully. Is one successful launch for every ten Stage IV cancellations (a 1:10 ratio) acceptable, or should the ratio be 1:3? It all depends. This is a matter of great subjectivity and variability between companies, investment and risk level, and industry type. However, what is not being questioned and measured can never be improved.

The Causes of Failure

On the surface, there are numerous primary causes. Another Product Development Management Association study cited the following as the main reasons for failure:[16]

- Lack of understanding of the market and customer
- Failure to commit the necessary resources to product development
- Lack of solid market research
- Lack of senior management engagement
- Moving targets

Another interesting study, a postmortem of 21 venture failures at 12 large multidivisional firms, revealed a number of practices that had a high degree of correlation with failure, such as the inability to meet budget guidelines or the lack of distribution channels. [17] In this study, *failure* was defined as any situation where the venture was terminated before full-scale commercialization was reached. The study separated the responses by those provided by top management of the company versus those provided by the new venture initiative management. Usually, they disagreed on most of the causes, such as if the venture or budget was too small or if there was a lack of sufficient authority.

In analyzing both of these studies, although the factors mentioned can and are contributors to failure, one should consider the following:

- There can be many subcategories/definitions for each (e.g., what exactly constitutes "lack of sufficient authority?").
- These causes vary by industry, company, competitive environment, market situation, and management.

- Failure is often due to multiple causes, each contributing to it in varying degrees.
- Many of these causes are highly correlated with each other (e.g., "lack of understanding of the market and customer" and "lack of solid market research")
- They can be highly subjective and possibly biased. In the venture management survey none of the venture managers cited "wrong venture manager" as a cause for failure, whereas it was observed six times by company management. In the opposite situation, none of the corporate managers cited "insufficient top management support" as a cause, whereas it was noted on eight occasions by venture managers.
- Although managers are often aware of these dangers, they often dismiss them as something that "wouldn't happen here," which can be a deeply embedded overconfidence bias.

These studies are mentioned in part to illustrate the fact that they are focusing on the most immediate or proximate causes and obtained through the inherently flawed survey approach. There is no substitute for applying one of the most successful and time-proven techniques, a root cause analysis, to identify the true contributors to failure in a product or company. Moreover, these root causes need to become part of the data collection activities required for any failure-reduction initiative, early warning system, or mitigation program, as described in later chapters.

Why Is Failure So Prevalent?

The underlying reason failure is so prevalent is because launching, marketing, and selling a product or service is extremely complex and the marketplace increasingly competitive. There are potentially thousands of options from which to choose in a business, marketing, or sales plan, so finding the optimal combination is extremely difficult. Many think this is an exaggeration, but that is symptomatic of how unaccustomed managers are to evaluating more than two or three options. Table 1.3 shows how many combinations or marketing programs are possible if one evaluates just eight variables and three options for each of these variables.

Table 1.3 Example of Possible Media Mix Options

Marketing Variable	Number of Options
1. Target market (e.g., seniors, females 21–25 with incomes over $30K)	3
2. Positioning	3
3. Advertising execution	3
4. Product packaging	3
5. Pricing	3
6. Distribution	3
7. Media mix	3
8. Promotion mix	3

The formula to find the total number of possible combinations is not 3 × 8 (or 24) different marketing mix combinations, but rather 3 to the 8th power, resulting in 6,561 options. This example uses a bare minimum of variables and options. If you considered additional variables, the number of combinations would increase exponentially into the billions![18] Anyone can now appreciate how very difficult it is for a company to pick the optimal combination.

Sophisticated companies, usually through agencies, are using market simulation software programs such as MARC Research's Assessor or Bases to identify the best combination of the marketing mix (e.g., price and packaging). Even though this software is a great asset to major companies, it is not available to everyone due to cost and the sophistication needed to correctly manage them. Moreover, its accuracy depends on the data and assumptions that are being entered by the business (e.g., Ore-Ida once did a simulation assuming that it would have a 90 percent distribution reach, but when it launched the product, it only obtained a 10 percent distribution reach[19]); as a result there is no guarantee that anyone will ever choose the optimal mix. Therefore, and as a safeguard, it is imperative for every company to establish an early warning system to quickly adjust course before the downward trend in a product or service becomes irreversible.

Final Thoughts on Failure

> *"I have not failed. I've just found 10,000 ways that won't work."*
>
> —Thomas Edison

As if matters were not complicated enough, many professionals rightly believe that some amount of failure is inevitable and is even to be encouraged. After all, no failures could mean a company is taking few or no risks and is thereby missing out on many potential blockbusters and opportunities. There are also famous examples of so-called drop errors, whereby excellent product ideas rejected by one company were successfully implemented by another. A well-known example is Xerox's PARC group, which, in spite of inventing the Ethernet, the PC mouse, and the PC graphical interface, still failed to commercialize these blockbusters. Another famous example was when Ken Olsen, founder, chairman, and president of one of the leaders in computers and software, Digital Equipment Corp, stated in 1977 that "there is no reason anyone would want a computer in their home."

A relevant analogy for this conundrum is a company's customer credit policy. If too restrictive, there will be many customers who would have paid but were turned away. However, if the company's credit standards are too lax, it might incur huge losses. When viewed under this prism, you can see that the concept of tolerating and allowing for some failure is not incompatible with the premise of this book.

One concept embraced mainly by "techy" types of entrepreneurs is the rapid iteration approach, whereby instead of spending too much time fine-tuning or testing a product or service, it is better to be, say, 85 percent initially perfect and then over time make additional iterations and improvements to the product or service with adjustments based on market feedback and fixing bugs found along the way (e.g., version 6.0). There is merit to this approach, but the same objective can still be accomplished by better decision making and using a Failure Mode & Effects Analysis, and this rapid iteration approach is easier done in industries where scale/liability are not issues (e.g., a gaming app). This approach would not work in the aeronautical, chemical, pharmaceutical, or medical device industries. Moreover, there are many potential downsides to a blanket application of this approach. What if the imperfections that are either tolerated or overlooked lead the company or product to be perceived as shoddy and amateurish by a key 20 percent of your market that accounts for 80 percent of potential business? You will also be creating negative word of mouth in today's socially connected world, which can damage both your brand and the prospects of repeat business (e.g., Window's ME or Vista operating system).

Instead, this book demonstrates how to minimize this risk through better problem framing, failure mode and effects analysis, an early warning system, and root cause analysis. Using the credit analogy, it would be prudent to give a new company a modest credit limit that is monitored and adjusted periodically instead of denying them any credit or giving them a large credit limit.

Failure can also have benefits if and when its magnitude is controlled and the causes understood or leveraged in a different direction. For example, if a company launched several customer acquisition or new product launches every year and they all underperformed and their corrective action consisted of replacing their chief marketing officer and/or some relatively inconsequential variable(s) (e.g., the creative aspect) in the hope of doing better, would that make a difference? Maybe, but what if the root cause was a combination of web usability, logistical delays, and knowledge gaps in best practices and optimization techniques by its Marketing department? In that case, the cycle of failure and underperformance would continue unabated until these were identified and fixed.

Finally, it is important to mention the meritorious "Plan B" approach[20] of looking for other options or markets should a product fail or underperform, which is conceptually different from the post-launch product improvement iteration approach previously mentioned. Pharmaceutical companies such as Eli Lily know that approximately 90 percent of its experimental drugs will fail, so it has trained its researchers to look for alternative uses and markets. Many blockbusters have resulted from this approach, such as Evista, which is an osteoporosis drug that was the result of a failed contraceptive. Viagra's erectile dysfunction benefits were discovered as a side effect observed in a compound being evaluated for heart disease. In fact, this approach has proven successful for products as varied as Hanes, which had to find a different distribution outlet (supermarkets) for its Legg's pantyhose brand, and Beefeater Gin, which in England was a low-priced gin, but which found the lower-price position in the United States was a saturated market, leading it to target the upper end of the market with great success. We explore the Plan B type strategies in Chapter 6, "The Preplanned Exit Strategy."

Now that we have completed a reality check on the relatively high odds of failure, we can start the process of discussing techniques used in other domains to reduce the likelihood or impact of failure and underperformance, starting with frameworks and *failure mode and effects analysis* (FMEA).

2

Don't Start Off on the Wrong Foot

"If I had an hour to solve a problem, I'd spend 55 minutes thinking about the problem and 5 minutes thinking about solutions."

—Albert Einstein

Most competent managers follow best practices when launching a new product or service, including the market research, forecasting, segmentation, prototypes, and, if applicable, the Stage-Gate process, to name but a few. The same diligence applies to management when considering merging or acquiring a new business, the Marketing or Advertising department running a campaign, the Finance department when suggesting new investment options, or sales managers prospecting for new customers.

In all these cases, however, the most important step is frequently skipped, an omission that often leads to a series of difficult-to-fix or unfixable outcomes. This error of omission is the tendency to jump in (action bias) using the wrong "frame" and without any controls in place to reduce or mitigate failure or underperformance. This chapter introduces a better decision-making process and proposes the domain transfer of a technique widely used in engineering and mission-critical process-intensive disciplines such as healthcare: *failure mode and effects analysis* (FMEA, pronounced "femea").

The Action Bias

Evolution, especially during the formative periods of our species, made the human race prone to *act* rather than *reflect*. This makes sense, given that those who didn't react swiftly to a noise behind them often didn't survive. There wasn't much deliberation or engaged, thoughtful thinking. As a consequence, people usually look at action more favorably than inaction, even if the outcome ends up being unfavorable.[1] For example, if a large company has a stagnant growth rate and a manager attempts a remedy that makes no difference whatsoever, he is more likely to be forgiven than a manager who took no action at all. In fact, the manager who took no action might even be fired. What if the action-oriented manager spent $15K on his poorly thought-out scheme? He is still more likely to be forgiven; that is the action bias at work.

It is therefore understandable that owners and managers feel obligated to take action. After all, it is their job responsibility. It's in their business DNA. Once this bias is understood, the best remedy is to devote a larger percentage of our time thinking about the problem and examining as many options as possible before jumping in. Moreover, one of the options should always be to do nothing.

Frames

"If all you have is a hammer, everything looks like a nail."

—Abraham Maslow

Frames are social constructs we create to simplify decision making in our personal and professional lives. In our personal lives, we frequently, and often without realizing it, use heuristic (rule-of-thumb) frameworks to simplify decision making (e.g., price is my most important consideration, so I usually buy the store brand). This behavior is very reasonable. If we had to deliberate and analyze numerous options before making any decision, virtually nothing would get done. The flipside is that in today's complex society, this instinctive or gut-based thinking can become a liability. This phenomenon was explained by economics Nobel Prize winner Daniel Kahneman in *Think Fast, Think Slow.*[2] The Think Fast (or Type I) approach is more "gut-based," whereby we are functioning on a type of "automatic pilot." The other type of thinking is the Think Slow (Type II) approach, which is more deliberative. When deciding which restaurant to eat at, we might engage the Type I or Think Fast approach, but when calculating a complicated math problem, most of us would use the Type II or Think Slow approach.

Although there is a logical reason for the existence of both types of thinking, the problem occurs when, often and without realizing it, we overuse and default to Type I thinking even in complex business endeavors. Usually, the typical professional framework is created based on one's likes, strengths, areas of expertise, experience, and company culture. While the default professional frame might be more complex than a simple heuristic, the problem or trap is that once created it tends to be used over and over again. People tend to select which business framework to use based on gut-based Type I thinking, even if the frame itself is complex and was created using Type II thinking. This is why it is so hard to see the trap; we marvel at how sophisticated our frame is instead of questioning whether it's even the right frame to use in the first place.

For example, if advertising and sales professionals are presented with the same business problem (e.g., declining revenues), the advertising person will gravitate toward advertising as the solution, whereas the salesperson will probably focus on prospecting. Here's another example: If sales are declining for a frozen food company, the Analytics department might overheat a few server processors trying to identify the cause and propose remedies, such as a pricing, promotion, or new channel partner, when the problem might be that they recently hired lousy food tasters and replaced some ingredients. The analytics manager may have come to believe that because he or she has literally hundreds of variables from which to analyze, such as financial and operational metrics, that the answer had to be somewhere in those gigabytes of data. As it turned out, this "soft" variable of "taste" was not one he or she had ever considered because it wasn't part of the usual operating framework. We cover this omission problem and how to avoid it in Chapter 5, "Blind Spots and Traps."

Consulting companies like McKinsey, the Boston Consulting Group, and Bain are among the few business entities skilled in identifying what the right framework should be for a given situation, which is the key: identifying what is the right framework instead of just applying the "usual" framework.

Framework Selection

When a request is made to conduct a major initiative such as launching a campaign or new product, try thinking through and analyzing numerous options, as highlighted in Figure 2.1, along with a case study example in Table 2.1.

You must first avoid the action bias and reflect on the crux of the issue or problem instead of jumping to some proposed solution. Usually, less than 1 percent of management time is spent on this key area. Next, proceed to identify the "default" framework being embraced and compare it against the core issue. Is it too narrow or the wrong framework? List all the implicit and explicit assumptions that were made and determine if these assumptions are based on verified facts or merely opinions and beliefs.[3]

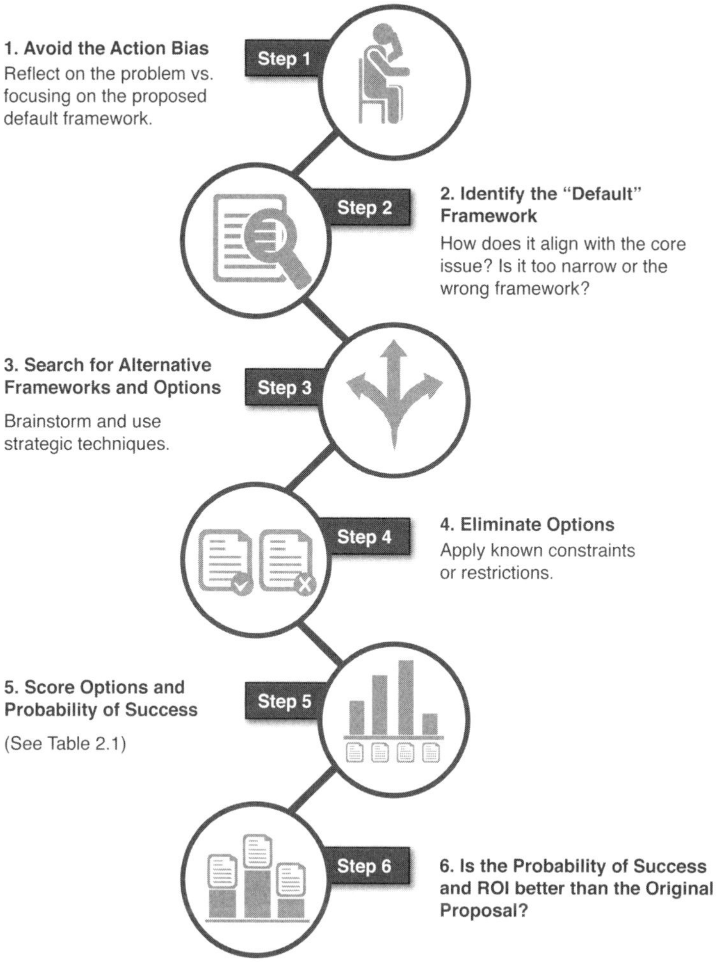

Figure 2.1 Selecting the right framework

The goal is to prove or disprove the initial framework by comparing it against other options. This approach mimics the statistical use of a null and alternative hypothesis—trying to disprove the usual framework. Next begin the search for alternative frameworks and options. Brainstorm and use strategic techniques such as the Ansoff matrix to come up with creative and alternative options. (For those not familiar with Ansoff's matrix, it categorizes opportunities by putting the potential options into four quadrants: existing customer and products [market penetration]; existing customers and new products [product development]; new customers and existing products [market development]; and new customers and new products [diversification].)

Next, eliminate options by applying known constraints or restrictions before proceeding to gather information on each remaining option's viability, chance of success, cost, and so on. Assign a probability of success and profitability to each option. This can be a sophisticated or simple model, such as the one shown in Table 2.1. The last step consists of making sure that the proposed solution has a higher probability of success and *return on investment* (ROI) than the original option. Did you prove or disprove the null hypothesis (the usual framework)?

Table 2.1 Framework Analysis Example

The Typical Approach

Tom, the VP of Sales for Elektra, a retail electronics manufacturer, pointed out in the yearly planning session that while the company had $110 million in sales, its growth rate had been anemic at only 1 percent per year. Tom recommends an aggressive customer acquisition campaign within the United States at an estimated cost of $500,000, which he feels sure would be very successful. Jack, a veteran CEO with 25 years at the company, trusts Tom and has given him the go-ahead. James, the new VP of Marketing, is asked to implement a marketing campaign that will bring in these leads.

Despite the ambiguity in many of the statements, the typical response from the VP of Marketing would be to assemble a team and begin the planning and information gathering process for an acquisition campaign. This automatic response typifies the Type I thinking approach, the action bias error, and applying the default "acquisition" framework based on the CEO's cue.

A Better Approach

The VP of Marketing should instead tell his team, "Let's not start just yet with the acquisition campaign. It appears that the crux of the issue is the lack of growth. The proposed framework is customer acquisition, but isn't this approach perhaps too narrow? Let's look at other options and collect data around each one."

The search for alternative frameworks yielded the following options:

1. Continue with the original proposal (the null hypothesis) by conducting a new customer acquisition campaign with the existing product line (Ansoff's matrix market development option).

2. Do nothing.
3. Focus on customer retention.
4. Increase the frequency and size of current customer orders (market penetration).
5. Launch a new product line for existing customers (new product development).
6. Launch a new product line for new markets (diversification).
7. Expand internationally.

The following restrictions exist: the amount of time and spending required for any new product line (R&D, testing, etc.) is not an option per the CEO. Moreover, the CEO has also ruled out going international. These factors eliminate options 5, 6, and 7. After gathering some information and assigning probabilities of success, profitability, and benefits to the remaining options, the following compensatory model was created:

Choosing the Right Framework

Options	**Key Facts Backing Up Likelihood of Success/ Growth Scores**	**Projected Growth**	**ROI of Promotion**	**Likelihood of Success**	**Total Score**
1. Conduct the customer acquisition campaign with our existing product line.	Used historical data of past acquisition campaigns and expert opinion from an agency and managers. It is also not a growth market but more of a zero-sum game, where any discounting or aggressive acquisition will lead to competitive retaliation and a price war based on experience.	.4(2)	.3(2)	.3(2)	2.0
2. Do nothing.	The CEO is very unhappy with the status quo. Not an option.	.4(1)	.3(1)	.3(1)	1.0
3. Customer retention.	The team discovered that the defection rate at Elektra is 12 percent per year versus the industry average of 5 percent. After some additional research, identified three reasons—billing errors, customer service hours and long hold times—all of which can be fixed relatively quickly.	.4(3)	.3(4)	.3(4)	3.6

Options	Key Facts Backing Up Likelihood of Success/ Growth Scores	Projected Growth	ROI of Promotion	Likelihood of Success	Total Score
4. Increase the frequency and size of current customer orders.	Our products have a cap on how much they can be used per year and are already close to the peak; any incremental gain will be very small.	.4(1)	.3 (3)	.3(2)	1.9

Note: The first value (e.g., 4) is the importance weight that you think that specific dimension (e.g., projected growth) should have; the weights should all add up to 1.0. The other value that appears in parenthesis is the rating you assign that dimension on a scale of 1–5 or 1–10.

For this type of model to be meaningful, each rating should have a scale; the following is an example for some of the factors:

Rating	Growth Rate from the Initiative	Return on Promotion* of Initiative	Probability of Success
1	Less than 1 percent	Less than 1 percent	Less than 20 percent
2	1–3 percent	1–5 percent	20–39 percent
3	4–6 percent	6–15 percent	40–59 percent
4	7–9 percent	16–25 percent	60–79 percent
5	Over 9 percent	Over 25 percent	80 percent or higher

The conclusion is that option 3—conducting a retention initiative—with a score of 3.6 out of 5 is both the safest option and the most likely to have a positive ROI. Moreover, until the customer defection problems are fixed, what is the point of bringing in more clients when they are being lost faster than they are acquired? Once the defection rate is brought down to industry standards, the original proposal can be re-examined, but even then a new analysis should be done about the best way to handle prospecting, given how the facts on the ground are always changing.

The Domain Transfer of Failure Mode and Effect Analysis

Once the correct framework is selected, the next challenge is to improve the odds of success given the high probability of failure or underperformance in any business venture. In this step, try to anticipate what can go wrong using the time-proven inductive framework of a FMEA. Inductive analysis is forward-thinking logic whereby you determine possible consequences from an event. The opposite, deductive analysis, is where you start out with an event (e.g., a failure) and work backward to find the cause. This deductive approach will be examined in Chapter 3, "The Business Failure Audit and the Domain Transfer of Root Cause Analysis." Both methods are inexorably intertwined. In the inductive FMEA, one component is to identify possible causes, which in turn are best identified by the deductive *root cause analysis* (RCA) process.

The key benefit of a FMEA is in identifying risks you did not realize existed, prioritizing the risks, and creating a blueprint for corrective action. The corrective action can take many forms, from modifying or adding additional detection controls to modifying the campaign, product, or service itself.

Brief History of FMEA and Its Adoption by Different Disciplines

The first known use of FMEA was by the Department of Defense in 1949 to analyze potential problems in the product design of tanks, artillery, and other critical weapon systems. FMEA was refined over time to include different FMEA types such as a *design* (DFMEA—i.e., new products) and *process* (PFMEA), which in our context would be a marketing campaign. The key difference between a process and a design FMEA, aside from the category, is that the team performing the FMEA will consist of different professionals and functional areas. In the DFMEA (new product or service), there should be representatives from R&D and Manufacturing, neither of which is needed in a PFMEA when used for a marketing or sales type of campaign.

Since 1949, FMEA has been extensively used by the military as well as other governmental agencies. The process of a FMEA domain adoption by nongovernmental entities and disciplines began in the mid-1970s. The trigger was a series of design and decision-making errors at Ford during the development of the Pinto automobile. These errors resulted in the explosion of several Pinto gas tanks during rear-end collisions and the deaths of more than 25 individuals. The exact number has always been in dispute, with some reporting it to be as high as 200.[4] A subsequent review conducted by Ford determined that these design errors would probably have been identified if a failure-detection methodology had been in place.

Given that FMEA was being used by engineers in the military and NASA, it did not take long for engineers in the automobile industry to embrace the FMEA technique. Soon after, it was adopted by most manufacturing industries, and especially by those manufacturing "mission-critical" products (e.g., telecom or medical devices). FMEA is also used extensively by healthcare, which has its own customized HFMEA. Along with RCA, the use of a HFMEA is a mandatory requirement for healthcare accreditation purposes by the *Joint Commission on Accreditation of Healthcare Organizations* (JCAHO). As evidence of the widespread acceptance and use of these techniques, approximately 82 percent of the nation's hospitals are JCAHO accredited.

However, despite the widespread adoption of FMEA, one recent incident initially baffled me. How can there still be such colossal failures as the 2014 General Motors ignition switch problem that resulted in at least 13 deaths and the recall of millions of GM cars? Closer examination revealed that in addition to outsourcing their parts manufacturing to suppliers, car makers have also outsourced the corresponding FMEA work to those suppliers. Experts on this topic state that FMEAs have "virtually disappeared from the car makers' engineering community and [have] been used as a weapon to beat concessions from suppliers and transfer liability to them."[5]

In the GM ignition switch case, industry analysts believe that the bad blood between General Motors and Delphi led to substandard parts being shipped by the supplier despite the fact that potential errors had been identified as a risk through a FMEA and verified as a problem by an RCA.[6] A similar situation occurred with faulty airbags manufactured by Takata; a U.S. congressional panel discovered, based on Takata internal emails, that global safety audits had stopped for financial reasons during a two-year period.[7]

It only requires a stroke of the pen to lower the probability of occurrence or the severity of a failure in an FMEA or hide the findings from an RCA if pressured to do so by management. These are realities and human follies that no FMEA or RCA can resolve.

Objectives of the FMEA

The FMEA is meant to identify, evaluate, and prioritize risks to reduce and prevent failure. To be effective, a FMEA must be customized (especially with the scales used for the severity, occurrence, and detectability ratings) to your company's specific challenges, objectives, and environment. I have tried to summarize and simplify the FMEA as much as possible while still covering its key components in a business context.

Best Practices for a Successful FMEA

- **Integrity:** Upper management must provide support and cover to those conducting the FMEA from pressure by interested or affected parties.
- **Burden or routine:** Approaching the FMEA as a burden or routine task will render it useless. A FMEA requires input from many different parties to be successful. Moreover, every new

product or campaign is different from previous ones because either the environment or a component will have changed.

- **Specificity:** The FMEA will not work if the function or failure modes being analyzed are too high-level (e.g., our marketing and sales initiatives this quarter). In fact, each major component of a campaign needs to be broken down within the FMEA (e.g., for example, if the lead generation campaign consists of both direct mail and advertising). Independent FMEAs should be done when the function is different.
- **Team:** A multidisciplinary team is needed in companies or situations when there are numerous departments and teams involved in the initiative being analyzed.

Components That Make Up a FMEA

Conducting a FMEA requires an understanding of its key components and their definitions. For example, if you confuse a mode with a cause or an effect, you might not be able to correctly determine the risk level. Figure 2.2 provides a high-level overview of the core components being covered.

Step 1. **Functions:** Identify the basic and secondary functions of the design (new product) or process (campaign) being analyzed. A function is basically what the product or process is supposed to do. There is usually only one primary function (a few at most) and several secondary functions.

For example, if a large electronics retailer is conducting a customer acquisition campaign, the basic function might be that the campaign generates a minimum of $1 million in profits to meet certain financial objectives, and a secondary function might be that the campaign does not exceed the established budget amount. In another example, this time for a financial software product, the primary function might be that it generates key ratio and financial calculations in compliance with SEC reporting requirements, with a secondary function that the software allow users to import financial data in many different file formats.

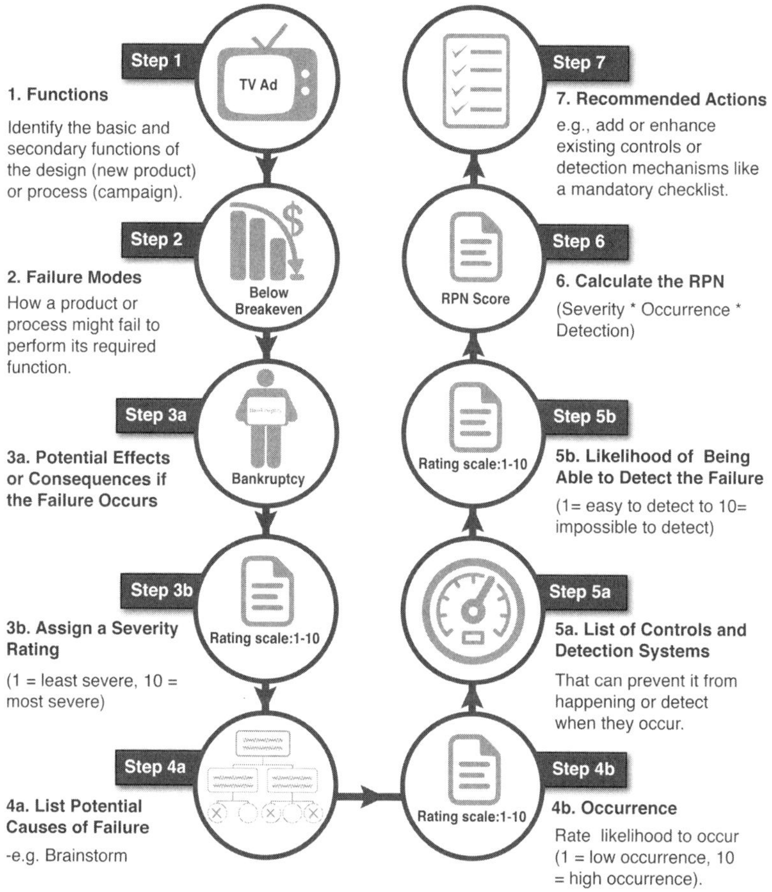

Figure 2.2 Flowchart of FMEA analysis

Determining the primary and secondary functions is usually pretty straightforward. The most common problem is when too many secondary functions are incorrectly classified as being primary. One way to distinguish between them is to remember that the secondary function makes the primary function faster, better, easier to use, and/

or more esthetically pleasing but is always still secondary in supporting and enhancing the primary function.

Step 2. **Failure Mode(s)** is how a product or process might fail to perform its required function. If the campaign has many subsets (email, direct mail, personal selling, etc.), you need to separate them out as subsections given each component will have its different effects and causes. Finally, the failure mode should be phrased as a negative statement, which can take on many forms, such as the following:

Process FMEA: If the direct mail portion of the campaign has a conversion rate that makes revenue fall below the financial profit target (primary function); as for the secondary function, if the cost of the campaign exceeds the budgeted amount.

Product or Design FMEA: The financial software does not correctly calculate the required ratios (the primary function); for the secondary function, if it cannot import a common data file format (e.g., a CSV file).

Step 3a. **Potential Effects from a Failure:** These are the consequences that could arise from the disruption of the related function. While every failure mode will have multiple effects, there should always be at least one main effect or consequence, such as the following examples:

Process FMEA for direct mail: As a result of the missed conversion rate, the department's monthly revenue target will not be met.

Product or Design FMEA for financial software: The customers file a lawsuit against the company for this misreporting error.

Step 3b. The Severity Rating: The next step is to assess, on a ten-point scale (1 = least severe, 10 = most severe), how severe the impact of this failure would be in your opinion if it were to occur.

- In the campaign example, you might assign a rating of 10 if missing the revenue target was so significant it could result in a decline of 5% or more in the company's stock price, and on the opposite end of the scale, you might assign it a rating of 1 if the impact is insignificant (given the relatively small size of the profit to be gained in comparison to the overall company revenue or profits). A best practice is to avoid assigning a rating of 1 to any effect because that may lull you into a false sense of security.
- For the financial software example, you might rate it a 10 if you believe the lawsuits could bankrupt your company, a 5 rating if lawsuits could amount to $500,000 or 25 percent of your annual profits, or on the extreme end of the scale, rate it a 1 if you think any penalties and awards from a lawsuit would be insignificant and easily settled out of court.

These rating scales do not have an absolute value and should be customized based on your company's specific needs, problems, and environment. Every company will have different tolerances and thresholds for monetary losses, breakeven, variances from forecast, revenue targets, and so on.

Step 4. Potential Causes of Failure: In this step, the FMEA tries to determine what caused the failure mode to occur. Coming up with probable causes can be done through the use of techniques such as those listed in Figure 2.3. (Although the causes suggested might be primary or secondary and not the root cause, for the purpose of the FMEA, that is fine.) Usually it will require a failure before you can truly uncover root causes.

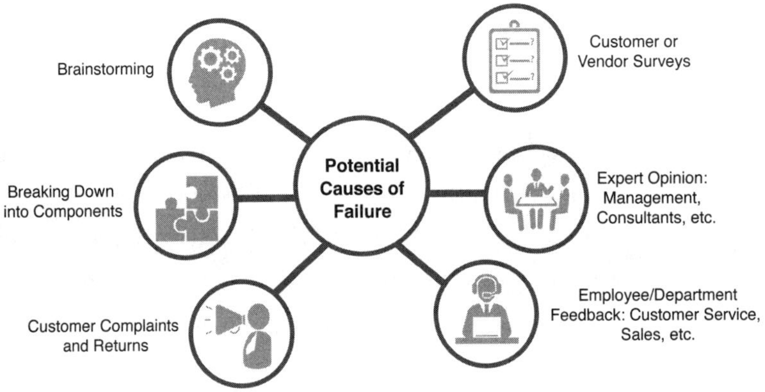

Figure 2.3 Useful techniques for the identification of causes of failure

Most of the methods listed in Figure 2.3 are self-explanatory; one could use more sophisticated techniques such as paired comparisons or nominal rankings to come up with additional causes, but these go beyond the scope of this book. However, the technique by which you break down a product or process into smaller components is a very powerful technique and thus worth elaborating on.

In this technique, you start out by breaking down the new product launch or proposed campaign into its different stages or components and then drill down into the specific details for each. (This technique is not an RCA per say, but rather a component of one; moreover, this technique can be used to find not just causes of failure, but also contributors to success). These micro-level components could be pulled from an existing product or campaign process flowchart and turned into potential problems. Figure 2.4 shows a brief example.

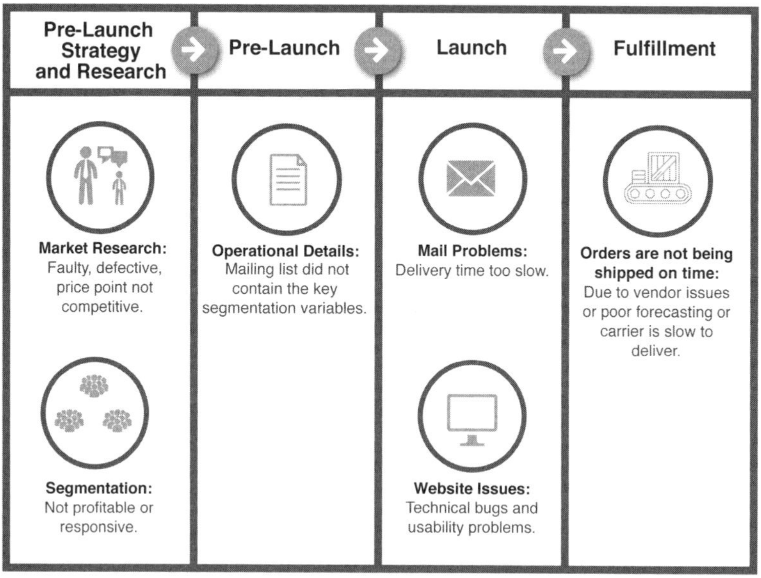

Figure 2.4 Breaking a task into smaller components to identify the possible causes of failure

Step 4b. Occurrence: Similar to the severity rating, you now need to rate on a ten-point scale how likely to occur this particular failure cause might be (1 = low occurrence, 10 = high occurrence).

- In the marketing campaign example, of a poor target market selection failure cause, you might rate the likelihood it will occur a 10 if you are very likely to pick the wrong target market given this is a new business venture and you have never conducted this type of campaign or segmentation; a 5 rating if you have great segmentation experience but not with this very dynamic and rapidly changing category; or rate it a 1, if you have an extensive record of success with segmentation analysis and picking the right target markets for this category.

- In the financial software example, you might assign the likelihood of its occurrence (for the potential cause of failure of a software bug in the calculations) a 10 if past versions always had some instance of this problem, a 5 rating if it might happen only with certain type of data sets, or a 1 rating if there is almost no chance this type of software bug can occur. (These assumptions are based on how comfortable you are with your existing controls and testing.)

  With any of these ratings, and especially with the occurrence scale (likelihood to occur), they should never be assigned a rating of 1. Companies tend to be overconfident about their abilities and chances of success, assuming that the worst will not happen. However, one only has to review the high rate of company and product failures to sober up on this matter.

Step 5. **Current Process Controls**: This consists of a listing of all the controls you currently have in place to prevent that particular failure cause from occurring or for detecting it once it does occur and before any significant damage is done. Controls are any kind of process, metric, or training you may have, such as checklists, protocols, mandatory testing, training, or instructions. Detection mechanisms are things such as the early warning system, which we cover in a later chapter, or if a product and your device contains alarms or gauges that alert for possible malfunctions.

Step 5b. **Detection:** In this step, you rate how easy is it for you to detect the problem or failure with your existing quality, risk mitigation, and failure-detection controls mechanisms (with the range being from 1 = easy to detect to 10 = impossible to detect).

- In the campaign example, you might assign a 1 to the potential failure cause of using an incorrect mailing list if your current controls could easily detect that failure cause or a 10 if it would be virtually impossible to detect, given that you use a vendor and as a result never see the list of names being used.
- For the faulty financial software ratio calculation example, if you could easily detect it through your current testing controls, you might assign it a 2, or a 10 if there is no way to detect the problem (which seems unlikely in this example).

Step 6. **The Risk Priority Number:** In this step, you multiply the ratings you assigned to the three different components to arrive at what is called the *risk priority number* (RPN). This is calculated as follows: RPN = Severity × Likelihood of Occurrence × Likelihood of Detection. The RPN score can be as low as 1 (it is unlikely to ever be that low and thus not recommended) or as high as 1,000. The calculated RPNs should then be ranked in descending order, with those on the higher end being given the most scrutiny and analysis. Table 2.2 shows an example of the components described in these steps. Once a FMEA has been conducted, companies will often find that they were unaware of important and potentially devastating sources and causes of failure (in this example, with the printing and shipping delays, given they had no mechanism in place to know of delays [because the job was outsourced to a third party]).

Table 2.2 Snapshot of a FMEA

Process Function	Potential Failure Mode	Potential Effect(s) of Failure	Severity	Potential Causes / Mechanisms of Failure	Occurrence	Current Process Controls	Detection	RPN	Recommended Actions
Campaign to generate $1M in profits.	Conversion rate below the threshold needed to meet revenue and profit target.	Monthly revenue target missed.	5	Poor target market selection.	4	None.	4	**80**	Conduct split testing before full launch to validate targeting.
				Approval, printing, and mailing delays make coupon dates too close to expiration.	4	None.	8	**160**	Request that the agency that prints and mails postcards provide a schedule and inform us of any delays.
				Price point not competitive.	3	Market research group monitors variance in competitor prices.	4	**60**	Implement a mandatory checklist that includes an updated competitive price list and discounts/coupons the competition is using.

Step 7. Recommendations: Finding gaps and improving existing detection and control mechanisms.

The last step is to analyze the higher RPNs and the "current process control" and "likelihood of detection" columns. If there are no controls listed, the main priority is to identify which new controls should be implemented. Often, a company will have preventive measures for low RPN failure modes but none for the higher RPN values. Even if an RPN has a control listed, a thorough review or audit of these measures should be conducted given the higher impact that mode of failure presents.

The RPN score and identification of deficient or missing prevention and detection mechanisms is where the value of a FMEA resides. Usually, there aren't many if any checks and controls before a product or campaign is launched. Even less common is the scoring and prioritizing of these risks. If there is a review, it is usually done on an *ad hoc* basis and tainted by both the availability (using only available information) and recency bias (the idea that something which has happened recently will have a bigger effect or influence than something which has never occurred). New product launches usually have more of these controls in place, but obviously not enough or of the right type given the overall high failure and underperformance rates.

Management, however, should not be naive. If they simply ask managers or employees if they have controls and detection mechanisms in place, no manager in his or her right mind would say, "Wow, I don't have any." It's too embarrassing. In addition, what is the definition of *control* or *detection* being used? Most people will say yes, even if the control is a three-item mental checklist or a notation in project management software to do X, Y, or Z; and the detection mechanism is when a customer calls in a complaint. Instead, management should not only ask what controls and detection mechanisms are in place for each RPN, but also require a thorough review by several different parties tasked with looking for gaps. Existing controls need to be documented and evaluated by the team, especially the first time an FMEA is conducted. Also, any time a change is made, there should be a log book documenting all changes, including the date and the parties involved and affected.

Examples of Preventive Measures

Preventive measure are measures that are done before a failure manifests itself. Common preventive measures for the proposed business FMEAs are the use of mandatory checklists, training, redundancy checks, audits, benchmarking, and testing. Figure 2.5 provides an overview of what the different preventive and detection mechanisms are.

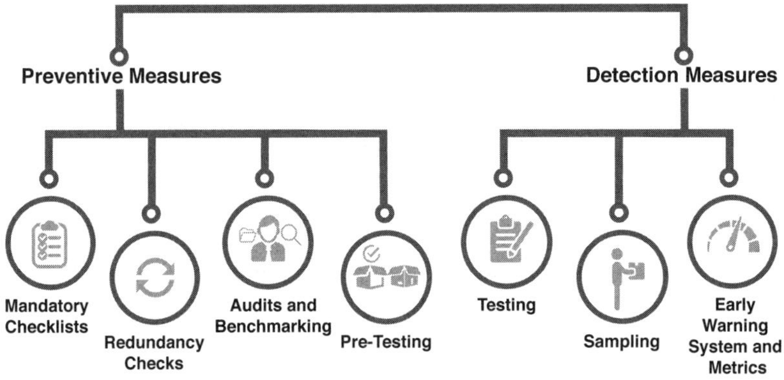

Figure 2.5 Examples of preventive and detection measures in a FMEA

- **Mandatory checklists:** These are probably one of the simplest and most important preventive measures. Requiring the use of a checklist seems simple enough, but despite their proven effectiveness, they are seldom mandated in business. For product launches, it is very much a hit-and-miss landscape, with some companies having a launch team that meets weekly to go through the project timeline and detailed checklist, whereas others meet infrequently if at all. In major companies skilled in new product launches, there is a specific team that handles only launches regardless of the product; at other companies, it is an ad hoc team. However, most small and medium-sized companies do not do anything even remotely close to that. So although checklists are common knowledge and understood, they are rarely mandatory or scrutinized for gaps and ways to improve them. The book *The Checklist Manifesto*[8] documents the value of this very simple technique and, without calling it such, proposes it as a domain transfer into disciplines that do not currently use them. That book cites that the first known use of a checklist as part of a mandatory protocol began with aviation in 1935 after a military plane crash and killed two highly skilled pilots; the cause was ruled as due to human error. The new planes had more engines, adjustments, and hydraulic controls, one of which had a locking mechanism that the pilot failed to disengage before takeoff. Shortly thereafter, the military created and mandated a *pilot's checklist* and empowered the copilot to stop the takeoff if he thought any of the steps were being overlooked or improperly done—a seismic shift in authority. Given the complexity of flying, leaving these preflight checks to the mercy of someone's memory was no longer a viable option.

At first, given the prevailing macho culture, the checklist was received coolly by aviators, but its value soon became apparent, given the deadly consequences from a careless mistake or omission. Today we see checklists used extensively by aviation, the military, major building construction projects, and NASA. Wherever complexity exists, checklists should be mandatory.

So why not adopt and apply this domain transfer (a mandatory checklist) to other professions such as medicine, where death or serious bodily injuries can be the end result when something is done or not done? Having to use a checklist was and still remains something that some physicians see as an affront and challenge to their competence. That the process is usually conducted by a nurse who may have even been given the authority to stop the procedure from continuing only makes matters worse. However, in 2001, Johns Hopkins Hospital decided to create and mandate a checklist to reduce persistently high rates of infection from intravenous lines. The result was that the ten-day "in-line" infection rate went from 11 percent to *0*. In one hospital alone, the use of a checklist prevented 43 infections and 8 deaths, saving $2 million in the process.[9] Checklists have achieved great success whenever complexity and multiple steps are required. They improve memory, focus, and consistency, and offer a baseline one can go back to if something was left off the checklist.

Returning to the less-hazardous business world, the use of mandatory checklists is also important given the high rate of failure and subsequent costs in terms of money and jobs. Very often, one omission (e.g., failure to verify whether the target segment was profitable or had a good response rate history) can make or break a campaign or product.

- **Redundancy checks:** Closely related to mandatory checklists are redundancy checks. Most occupational accidents and deaths occur due to complacency. Jailers, construction workers, and electricians probably perform certain high-risk tasks hundreds or thousands of times over a period of years, eventually becoming more and more risk tolerant or even blind to risk, which is when the accidents or tragedies are more likely to occur. It is no different in business. A manager who has been involved with the launch of a new product or campaigns for months will, after the tenth iteration, start to gloss over critical steps or overlook red flags. The checklist might be glanced at and performed in 3 minutes when it should take more like 30 minutes when done correctly, checking each element carefully for correctness and accuracy. The best preventive measure for this problem is to establish a layer of redundancy by having someone else go through the checklist, confirming proper training is being done and that prelaunch testing, if applicable, has been completed.

- **Training and domain knowledge:** If a manager is tasked with conducting market research for a new business initiative and the manager lacks expertise in this area and relies solely on social media, focus groups, or opinions, you have a recipe for disaster that most checklists will not pick up on. Some of the most common root causes of business failure are a lack of training, knowledge deficiencies, or the lack of a written process. An individual manager's domain knowledge and expertise is usually not questioned by management unless something bad happens; companies assume that if someone was hired for a function like marketing, sales, or finance, that this person must be competent. He might be, but perhaps not in the specific area to which he is now being deployed. Marketing, for example, is a big umbrella that covers specialties such as event management, analytics, public relations, lead generation, direct, and digital, to name just a few. Even within a specialty like digital, someone who has only done social media marketing would be unqualified to conduct a pay-per-click and web analytics task, and vice versa. Moreover, how is proficiency measured? Perhaps your pay-per-click campaign gets a 3 percent conversion rate, and you are happy because breakeven is at 2 percent, but what if more talented professionals are regularly getting above an 8 percent conversion rate?

  The training preventive measure is to make sure your people are getting the correct and latest training in their field. In today's business environment, this means being well read on current topics in their domain, taking additional courses, and probably taking some type of software training, including a basic statistics and advanced spreadsheet course. Another preventive measure would be to test their domain knowledge expertise, which might start with the area manager. That person may have been promoted based solely on merit, but perhaps his or her skills have not kept up with new emerging areas or technologies. If there is no training or measurement of an employee's domain knowledge gaps, this is a preventive measure that needs to be addressed, especially if linked to high-risk, high-impact RPN areas.

- **Audits and benchmarking:** Conducting a functional area audit is another possible preventive measure. The next chapter covers this in more detail and also explains why they are not used much. When conducted, these functional area audits are comprehensive and look at components such as training, software, and processes. In any case, the FMEA is a quicker and more practical tool than the functional area audit.
- **Pretesting:** This refers to testing that should take place before a product is launched. While the tests can be the same in the pre- and post-launch phases, usually the prelaunch testing is more internally restricted (although it can include consumers or customers in a beta test), whereas the post-launch testing usually focuses solely on consumers or customers. In the prelaunch testing, you are trying to accomplish preventive measure objectives such as the following:
  - For a new product or service: Identify bugs by stress testing. For example if your website is projected to handle 300 transactions per day, see what happens if 3,000 concurrent transactions are taking place. (Note that there is software for that type of simulated testing.) Conduct tests of every functionality to see how they work, their accuracy, speed, ease of use, and performance under different conditions and under different systems or environments (e.g., temperature ranges or operating systems), or the aesthetics (e.g., color, ergonomic design options).

- You may also be trying through tests to determine the demand for a potential new product or service, be it by targeting prospects and doing a small-scale launch or campaign to determine conversion rates.

Detection Measures

Detection measures are those that detect problems or failures after the product, service, campaign, or other major business initiative has started or launched. They include the following:

- **Testing:** These tests are, as mentioned earlier, done after the launch to monitor your product, campaign, or platforms (be they websites or call centers) to make sure that there are no problems, but also to optimize your product or campaigns. Ideally, any test conducted should, if possible, be statistically representative. The test can be of almost anything—testing a landing page URL once your campaign has started, conducting browser, mobile, and usability tests, determining whether the coupon code works correctly with different SKUs, measuring the average pick, pack, and shipping rate of your fulfillment center, timing and testing the average delivery time of any campaign material, and also for the products or services being sent.
- **Sampling:** For some activities, you should take random samples of orders that are being fulfilled to make sure that the product has been correctly picked from the shelf, packaged correctly to minimize damage, and labeled correctly for shipping purposes. Or, if you have a mailing list, collect samples by randomly pulling out every *n*th name and checking to make sure it matches the desired target market and that the label and postage are dimensioned to postal requirements.

- **Early warning system and metrics:** The last control is to make sure you have threshold metrics in place that can act as an early warning system, which is examined in great detail in Chapter 4, "The Early Warning System." An example of these metrics might be if customers are returning a higher-than-normal number of orders, the conversion or repeat purchase rate is below forecast, negative comments are showing up on social media, or if the hold times at your call centers are higher than normal.

Today the FMEA technique is ingrained into the DNA of engineering and in industries like healthcare and telecommunications as an essential tool to prevent or mitigate failure; it would be inconceivable to professionals in these fields that a FMEA would not be done for an important product or project. With business professionals, however, be they in marketing, finance, business development, sales, strategy, or product management, the norm is that most will have never even heard of a FMEA, let alone used it. Hopefully, the seed will be planted among the innovators and early adopter readers of this book so that it can become as pervasive and useful in business as it is in engineering.

3

The Business Failure Audit and the Domain Transfer of Root Cause Analysis

"Those who cannot learn from history are doomed to repeat it."

—George Santayana

Although business and campaigns often fail and underperform at great expense, most companies make no serious effort to determine the reasons why such failures occur. Usually, a department or manager is blamed, and they are either fired or their career is stalled. In other cases, if the department or person is lucky and well connected, or management is disengaged from day-to-day matters, the failure might be attributed to bad timing, the competition, or some other external factor. In addition, people have an innate tendency to look for external causes rather than question their own skills, abilities, or thinking. A study by Harvard showed that first-time entrepreneurs have only an 18 percent chance of succeeding and that entrepreneurs who previously failed have similarly low odds of success at just 20 percent. Clearly, one major reason for ongoing failure and underperformance is that people fail to learn from past failures.[1] There are three problems with the traditional approach companies take to identifying failure:

1. **The lack of a scientific methodology:** Companies arrive at their conclusions without the use of any consistent methodology or extensive analysis. Instead, it's usually based on anecdotal information, gut feeling, or office politics. Often, companies approach layoffs in this manner despite claims to the contrary. The people laid off might have been picked because they did not socialize with or were not as liked as others by management, as opposed to some measurable performance comparison.
2. **Blaming the proximate (or immediate) cause:** The other problem is that this approach only looks at the proximate causes to the failure (i.e., the manager or competition) and not at each of the contributing, intermediate, and root causes. The competitive response might be strong or the manager incompetent, but who failed to identify this scenario or deficiency? Moreover, there might be additional causes such as deficient or incomplete reports or studies provided to the manager by other departments. If so, what guarantee is there, if it is blamed on the incompetence of managers who are then fired, that subsequent managers won't have the same professional deficiencies and/or use deficient reporting or market research?
3. **A deeper hole:** Companies often take the "try harder" approach. The result is additional time and resources poured into a venture that might be doomed to failure regardless of the effort made. The company might be digging itself into a deeper hole instead of identifying and implementing the necessary changes or planning for an early and less-costly market exit. This has happened to small and large companies who think that by staying the course and redoubling their efforts things will change; but if you are lost and going in the wrong direction, this approach only gets you to failure sooner and poorer. The business landscape is littered with these cases such as Webvan or Pets.com.

How Should One Proceed? The Domain Transfer of Root Cause Analysis

If a product is not working or has a malfunction of unknown origin, it would be very time-consuming, costly, and possibly disastrous if the technician attempted to solve the problem using "gut feeling" or office politics instead of a deductive process that systematically went through a series of decision tree-type questions, with each answer determining the next path to follow until the solution is identified, as shown in Figure 3.1.[2] A similar process and best practice for cases where product, process, or system complexity exists and failure occurs is root cause analysis (RCA); RCA is the gold standard wherever complexity is present and failure occurs.

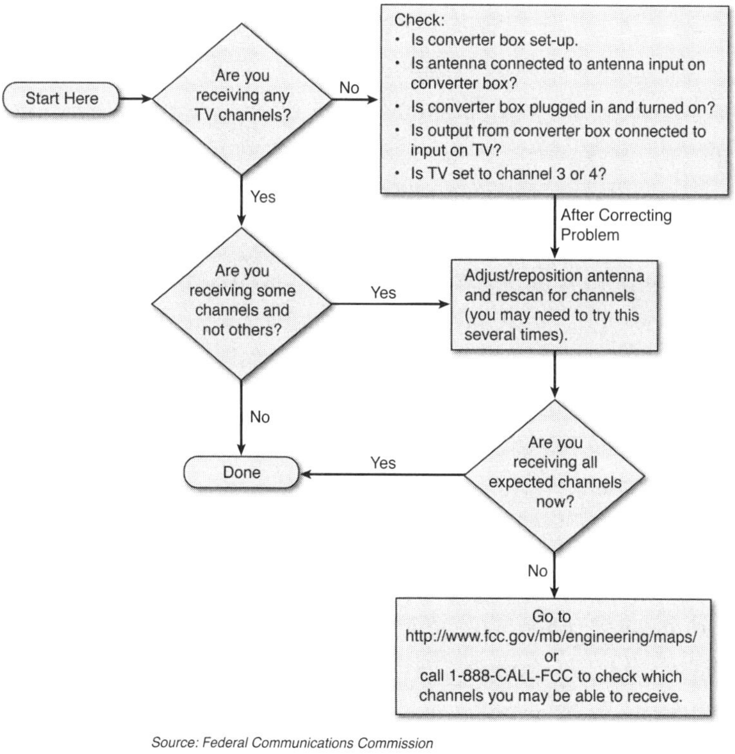

Figure 3.1 Example of a Troubleshooting Decision Tree (Source: Federal Communications Commission)

This chapter proposes a domain transfer of this technique to business, with some modifications and enhancements to create a business failure audit. However, before examining the proposed failure audit, it is useful to understand its origins and clarify the difference between a failure audit (after a failure occurs) and a functional area audit (no failure need have occurred), given that some companies, although few and far between, conduct the latter.

Differences Between an RCA and Functional Area Audits

The concept of business and functional area audits is based on the idea (like the accounting audit) that a company should periodically conduct a general or functional area audit of its people, processes, software, metrics, rewards, and compliance. The Small Business Administration has, for example, a business audit document used to analyze the management, operations, and financial areas of a company. Then there are the functional area audits; marketing thinkers and scholars have been strong proponents of this concept for several decades. The American Management Association introduced the "marketing audit" in 1959. Since then, there have been several articles and even a book on conducting marketing audits by authors such as Philip Kotler and Aubrey Wilson, both of whom detail the different areas that should be examined, including strategy, environmental scans, department structure, employees, customers, systems, budgeting, products, pricing, advertising, sales, and all the components that make up a typical marketing plan.

Conducting a functional area audit is a good idea given that it entails an in-depth examination of different functions to identify those areas that may require improvement. Benchmarking is a big component of any business or functional type audit. The failure audit being proposed, however, has a narrower focus, analyzing only the underlying root causes for a specific failure. The functional audit will probably not reveal what caused an initiative like an investment or campaign to fail, and the failure audit probably won't uncover other potential causes of failure if unrelated to those identified in the failure audit. The functional audit and failure analysis are thus different but complementary tools that should be used as part of any continuous improvement effort.

The functional area audit looks at the following general areas in a systematic and independent manner:

- **People:** Are they proficient in their work? Do they have solid domain knowledge (e.g., certifications)? Do they stay up to date with new technologies and changes in their profession?
- **Policies, procedures, and processes:** Does the area have these in place for important tasks and initiatives?
- **Software:** Does the area have the latest and appropriate tools to perform its duties effectively? Benchmarking is a key part of this aspect.
- **Metrics:** What are the success metrics by which the area is measured, and what additional metrics should it be measured against?
- **Rewards and compliance:** What mechanisms are in place to ensure that the company and area objectives are being achieved? When objectives are not being met, what corrective action is being implemented?

The Adoption of Functional Area Audits

As good as the functional area audit concept is, the reality is that most companies, including marketing, have not widely adopted the functional audit. When speaking with some of the largest advertising and marketing agencies, such as those that are part of the Wunderman and Omnicom conglomerates, the consensus is that they are rarely conducted.

There are many reasons for this low adoption rate. To many managers, the concept bears all the hallmarks of a fishing expedition; moreover, the average audit can take approximately five to ten weeks. Lean staffing at many companies means that they cannot afford to have key personnel tied up for days or weeks answering questions for an unknown payoff. Also, the thought process goes, if something is not broken, why try to find problems to fix? Calculating the *return on investment* (ROI) for a functional or business audit is very difficult on the front end. Moreover, what if the problems the audit uncovers are marginal and do not translate into an improvement in productivity, customer satisfaction, or profitability? A negative ROI is a possibility when a functional area audit is conducted on a company with strong growth and profitability. Another concern is whether those conducting the audit are really qualified to do so: If an outsider, do they have the internal domain subject expertise to ask the right questions and identify specific problems? If by an internal person, do they have the knowledge on how to conduct a thorough audit and have the necessary internal buy-in?

In fact, business audits are actually more commonplace than functional area audits and are usually conducted in Fortune 500 types of companies by outside consultants like Bain or McKinsey, who do it as part of the discovery needed to achieve a broader objective. These consultants are usually brought in when management has problems, such as low to negative growth, and are looking for strategic advice. Moreover, these business audits tend not be as detailed as functional area audits, in part because of the necessary domain-specific expertise, additional time, and cost that would be required.

Because of these challenges, the *Failure Mode and Effects Analysis* (FMEA) and RCA business failure audit are better and more practical alternatives than the functional area audit. For one thing, they avoid the objections that functional area audits tend to create. In the FMEA, you are focused on a key strategic initiative, such as campaign or product launch. In the failure audit, the company has already experienced failure for some major initiative, eliminating the fishing expedition scenario; moreover, the company is through the failure audit trying to prevent future occurrences of systemic failure. In addition, while a functional area audit might take several weeks to conduct and involve a large number of people, an RCA or FMEA can take a few hours or days at most, depending on the complexity of the problem and business.

Background and Use of the Failure Audit (Root Cause Analysis)

The systematic use of RCA is believed to have started more than 60 years ago, when engineers saw the need to troubleshoot defective products/equipment using a more consistent methodology. One, if not the first, adoption of RCA was by the *National Aeronautics and Space Administration* (NASA), which has since refined and developed additional subtypes of RCAs. RCA has expanded over the past few decades into almost every industry and scientific discipline, including healthcare, where an RCA is a requirement in an industry-wide accreditation program known as the *Joint Commission on Accreditation of Healthcare Organizations* (JCAHO).

Failure analysis can be categorized based on the subject matter, such as production-based, safety-based, process-based, and systems-based RCAs. Unfortunately, there is usually no standard protocol or set of methodologies in many of these RCA types, even though the techniques are all very similar. Because of this, I have mainly relied on the safety-based RCA, borrowing some procedural concepts from the *National Transportation Safety Board* (NTSB), but relying mainly on the RCA methodology used by NASA.

The NTSB, which was created in 1967, is responsible for investigating mass transportation accidents (i.e., train or aviation) within the United States. The NTSB uses rigorous protocols when an accident occurs to sort through all the possible contributors and parties involved until the "probable cause" of the accident is identified. However, while the NTSB offers many valuable lessons for business failure audits, it doesn't go all the way down to the root cause because it does not have any jurisdiction over private companies and their internal processes and products. For example, if a faulty ball bearing was identified as the probable cause of an airplane accident, the NTSB would stop their analysis after identifying the ball bearing, even though it is only the proximate or intermediate cause, as opposed to the root cause, which may have been that the procurement department was only looking for the cheapest part. However, the NTSB process contains several concepts that have been incorporated into the business failure RCA presented here, including the need to maintain the independence and integrity of the audit group and investigation, the free access to evidence, the identification and inclusion of key parties and investigative specialties (e.g., finance, sales, data analytics), and the discovery process by which interested parties can provide and challenge information obtained during the investigation.

NASA's RCA Methodology

NASA, unlike the NTSB, does conduct failure analysis down to the root cause because it owns and operates the aircraft and rockets that could be involved in a mishap. NASA has, unfortunately, experienced failures with significant national security, strategic, human, and financial consequences. These factors led NASA, especially after the latest Columbia disaster, to become the world authority in mishap investigations, developing a robust and ongoing failure analysis program currently managed by the Mission Critical and Assurance Division.[2] This group is responsible for producing numerous training manuals and whitepapers, analyzing failures, and benchmarking with other industries and government agencies.

How to Conduct the Failure Audit: An Overview

As is often the case with any tool, the failure audit has its limitations, and using it might not be warranted when insufficient data exists to uncover the root cause or the problem is either so simple or trivial that it does not warrant the time needed to conduct the failure audit. Figure 3.2 provides a good overview of the Failure Audit[3] (an additional and detailed example is provided in Figure 3.3). Please also note that each step has its set of constraints, guidelines, and metrics that lend themselves to further customization and refinement.

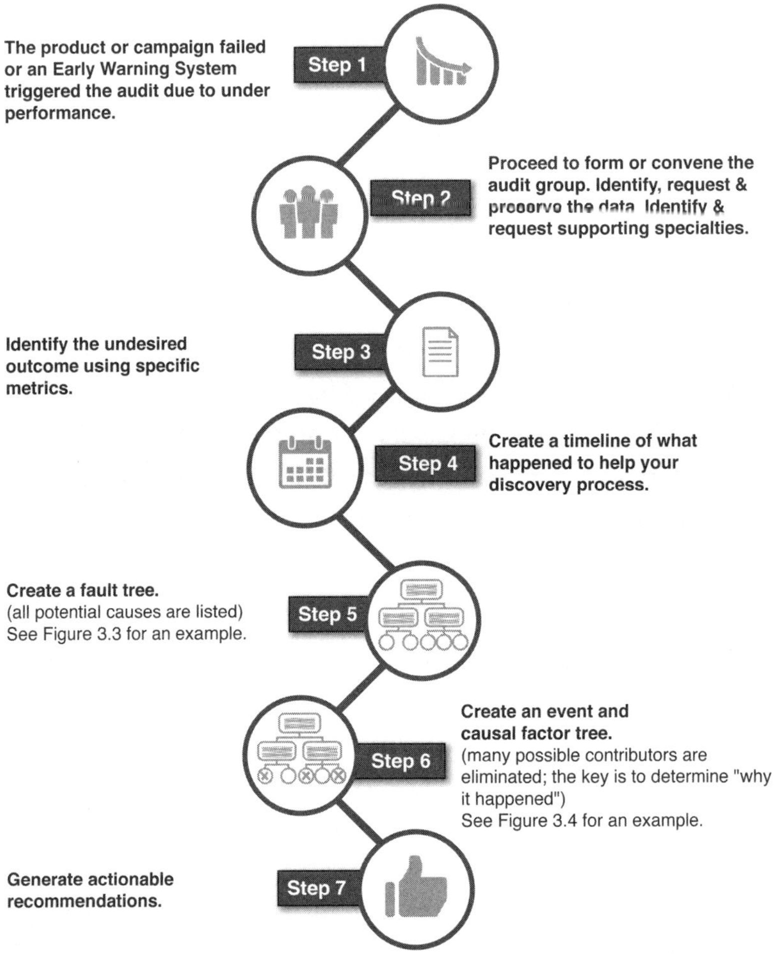

Figure 3.2 Summary of the proposed business failure audit

Most of the steps in the flowchart are self-explanatory. The RCA component takes place in step 5 (fault tree). In this step, you are creating a logic diagram, listing out all the possible faults that could have contributed to the undesired outcome. These can include things such as human error, competitive response, economic environment (recession), natural phenomenon (inclement weather), and so on. The objective is to list as many events as you can by using techniques such as brainstorming, nominal group, decomposing or breaking down into smaller components, gathering information from technical experts, interviewing those parties involved in the failed launch, and so on.

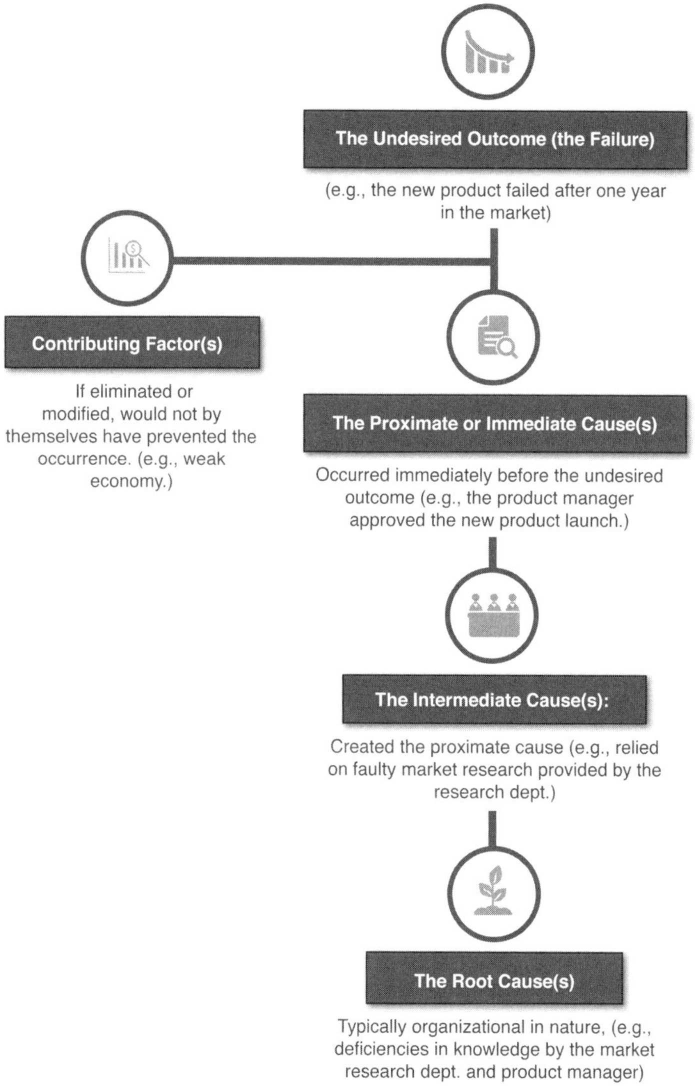

Figure 3.3 Overview of the fault tree

The Start of the RCA—The Fault Tree (Step 5)

A fault tree consists of the undesired outcome (failure) and proximate, intermediate, and root causes, as shown in Figure 3.3. (The example in Figure 3.3 is not a complete fault tree, but an abridged version so as to not clutter the diagram and to keep the focus on the components.) Because the root cause is the farthest down the causal chain from the undesired outcome, it is often difficult to identify unless an RCA is undertaken. Figure 3.4 provides a detailed example. During this stage, all the assumptions need to be carefully examined, looking for omissions or those that turned out to be incorrect. Once the fault tree in step 5 has been completed, creating the event and causal tree (step 6) is relatively easy and more of an exercise in eliminating and potentially enhancing several causes listed in the fault tree.

- **The undesired outcome (the failure):** This is the direct result of an action by somebody or something, usually due to several events and actions. The outcome must be very specific and provide metrics that quantify the failure:
  - The campaign had an average conversion rate of 0.1%, 70% lower than was needed to achieve break-even.
  - The new product was a failure with sales 80% below forecast during year one.
- **The proximate or immediate causes:** This includes the events that occurred immediately before the undesired outcome and led directly to the occurrence of the undesired outcome. The elimination of a proximate cause would prevent the undesired outcome:
  - The manager implemented and launched the lead generation campaign.
  - The product manager managed and approved the new product as it went through each step in the stage gate development process, including the launch.

— The price of the product was increased by 20% at the beginning of the first quarter.

- **Contributing factors:** These are events or conditions that may have contributed to the occurrence of an undesired outcome but, if eliminated or modified, would not by themselves have prevented the occurrence. Contributing factors impact the intensity of an undesired outcome. For example, the weak economy, a contributing factor, was not a major contributor to the failure but did have a role in aggravating the failure.
- **The intermediate causes:** These are events or conditions that created the proximate cause and which, if eliminated or modified, would have prevented the proximate cause from occurring. Often there may be one or several intermediate causes for a single proximate cause:

— The campaign used prospect names and addresses that did not match the target market.

— The product manager based his decision on market research provided by the research department and failed to conduct testing to validate the study's assumptions (two intermediate causes).

— The product manager did not take into account the competition when it set the new price and misinterpreted the price elasticity study (two intermediate causes).

- **The root causes:** These are usually several events or conditions, and typically organizational in nature, that contributed to or created the proximate/intermediate cause and subsequent undesired outcome, and which, if eliminated or modified, would have prevented the undesired outcome. For example, the product manager did not use a prelaunch campaign checklist to identify errors, or the marketing manager had no training or knowledge in key techniques commonly used in lead generation, such as testing, recency-frequency-monetary value, segmentation, or mailing list knowledge and selection:

— The product, marketing, and market research areas did not understand the role and limitation of focus groups, which was the basis of their research, and therefore failed to undertake a large and statistically significant survey, followed by testing, to validate the faulty assumptions upon which the product launch was based.

— None of the product or marketing areas had a comprehensive pricing methodology in place and the necessary skill set and training needed to correctly conduct and interpret elasticity studies.

Step 6: Creating the Event and Causal Tree

The main objective in this step is to eliminate as many of the events listed in the fault tree as possible. However, this should be done only if you have solid evidence that they did not cause or contribute to the undesired outcome. In the example shown in Figure 3.4, the proximate cause "inclement weather" was dropped when further analysis revealed that no other similar products suffered a loss in sales in that region. The other key task is to ask why each event or condition that was listed occurred. This helps you see whether that event can in turn be further deconstructed into smaller events. (See in Figure 3.4 how the proximate cause "dealing with the low purchase rates by the target market" is deconstructed into an intermediate cause of "a new and unproven target market was chosen.") This process can be enriched by using techniques such as relations diagrams, scatter charts, affinity diagrams, and other tools used in complex RCAs.

It is critical that the "why" question be asked over and over, at each step, until the root cause is reached. The RCA must continue until organizational-type factors are identified or all the available data has been exhausted. When asking why, establish if a cause-and-effect relationship exists. You will learn some techniques for determining whether a cause-and-effect relationship exists in Chapter 5.

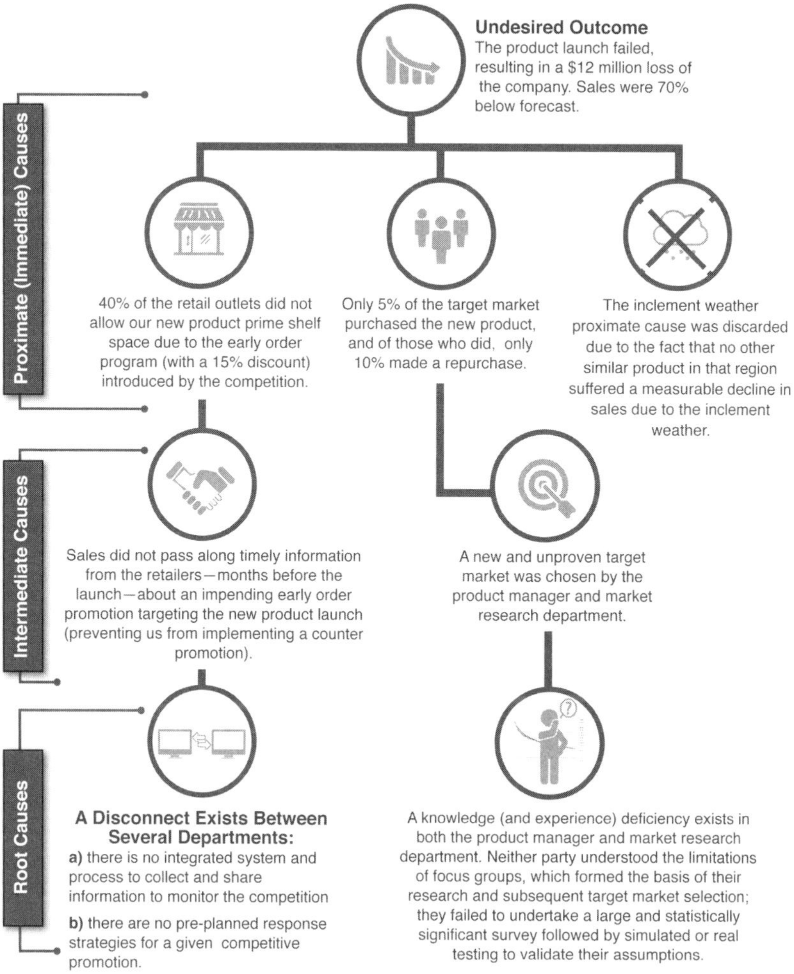

Figure 3.4 Transitioning from the fault tree into the event and causal tree

Step 7: The Final Recommendations

The final step requires the development of very specific recommendations. Because the objective of an RCA is to prevent the recurrence of the failure or undesired outcome, your recommendation should completely eliminate the root cause(s) problem. If the elimination of the root causes does not also eliminate or negate the recurrence of all the proximate and intermediate causes, you should include specific recommendations to eliminate these other causes. In your recommendations, you should mention, if applicable, the need for additional training, new talent hiring, more stringent sign-off and approval processes for different campaign stages, the creation of a special cross-functional team, the use of a mandatory prelaunch checklist, and so on. See the example in the following sidebar.

Sample Recommendations for Root Cause Problems

1. **Market Research:** The product manager needs additional and possibly outside training to make better segmentation and targeting decisions, ask the right questions, and identify potentially deficient research. The Market Research department may need a more complete overhaul given the knowledge deficiency demonstrated. Until the knowledge and experience deficiency is remedied—through training or additional or replacement hiring—any interim research should be conducted or supervised by a well-qualified outside market-research firm.
2. **Competition:**
    a. A manager should be identified and tasked with the creation and maintenance of a system to monitor the competition on an ongoing basis. This person should have access to all the sales call reports. The sales force should be instructed to provide details of all competitive activity taking place in their territory, making the timely

and accurate collection of this and other sales data a part of their review and bonus program.

b. Going forward, it should be required that all marketing and product launch plans incorporate a mandatory checklist for several key stages in the process and that more worst-case scenarios be incorporated (e.g., a strong competitive response) with a detailed plan indicating what counteraction should be implemented for a given time and place. For example, if the competitor's price is decreased by less than 5 percent, do nothing; if a 5 percent to 10 percent price decrease occurs, counter with a comparable but slightly lower discount or offer a bundled offer, free service, extended warranty, and so on.

In addition, an early warning system should be created using leading indicators so that more advanced warning can be given when product underperformance starts to manifest itself. In addition, an exit trigger should be created as well as a preplanned exit strategy with several options should the underperformance continue despite all remedial efforts.

All the affected individuals or areas should receive copies of the final report and be given the opportunity to document or present their rebuttal and comments. Note, however, that rebutting or commenting should never result in the watering down or changing of the conclusions because that can undermine the investigative team's efforts. The only exception to this could be if and when a major flaw is found in how the failure analysis was conducted. Any comments or rebuttals submitted should be appended to the report and passed on to management, who may then ask additional questions, request additional information or analysis, and decide who is correct.

In conclusion, if a company continues to not have a process to determine the root causes of a failure, it will keep repeating its errors and aggravating the problem. The gut-based or office politics approaches to assigning blame are unfair, institutionalize mediocrity, and lay the groundwork for future and possibly larger failures.

4

The Early Warning System

"Forewarned, forearmed; to be prepared is half the victory."
—Miguel de Cervantes, author of *Don Quixote*.

Situational awareness is a term used to define the need for heightened awareness of one's surroundings when entering an area of uncertainty or danger. In a business context, it is the ability to identify, process, and comprehend on an ongoing basis the critical elements of information about what can and is occurring. The purpose of this chapter is to raise situational awareness on a continuing basis among companies concerning our ever-present companions: failure and underperformance. Usually, managers have a heightened sense of awareness during the creation and initial stages of a new endeavor, but as soon as that is over, their focus naturally shifts to other matters, thereby reducing that heightened awareness.

Chapter 1, "Failure & Stagnation," revealed how in any major business endeavor, whether it be the launch of a new business, product, or a campaign, there can be literally thousands of different options to choose from, which makes finding the optimal combination very difficult. As a result, businesses need to monitor those signals that provide the earliest possible warnings about emerging problems. If you are in a *business-to-business* (B2B) industry and selling equipment with a sales cycle measured in months, you may find yourself in irreversible trouble if you wait for revenue metrics. Traditional outcome metrics, such as revenue or market share, are obviously necessary, but these should not be the key drivers of an *early warning system* (EWS). Instead, you need to identify other variables that provide more advanced warning.

Background

In our daily lives, we see the widespread use of EWSs that provide advanced notice to prevent negative outcomes. Gauges on our cars are constantly measuring the engine temperature, oil, and gas levels. This might appear to be stating the obvious, given that we also have business dashboards that capture metrics like the number of orders, revenue, profitability, and so on. Although that is true, the majority of metrics used in business dashboards are *lagging* (e.g., revenue) instead of *leading* indicators (e.g., awareness). In addition, not all leading indicators are equally good. Some are critical success drivers, whereas others just add to the clutter. To finish with the car analogy, we tend to have on business dashboards gauges with lagging indicators, such as the check engine light, which appear when something has already malfunctioned. Some business areas, such as web analytics, make good use of leading indicators, including them as *key performance indicators* (KPIs), but they rarely separate them out from lagging indicators, prioritize, classify them as short term versus long term, or forecast what numbers they expected, all of which are important components of the EWS.

Finance has been using a type of early warning mechanism for years, which is the *Z-score.* This score was introduced in 1968 by Edward Altman, a New York University finance professor, to predict the likelihood that a publicly traded manufacturing company might find itself in a state of bankruptcy 12 to 24 months before that event (whether the company actually takes the legal step of declaring bankruptcy is, of course, another matter). Altman subsequently introduced a *Z-score plus* and *double-Z prime* versions for use on privately held and nonmanufacturing companies. In tests over a 30-plus year period, the Z-score was found to be 80 percent to 90 percent accurate in predicting bankruptcies one year prior to the event.[1] Bond rating agencies like Moody's use a similar methodology, weighing many different factors; however, some of the factors are subjective (e.g., management expertise). While subjective factors may be necessary, the fact that many of the companies being rated, such as Countrywide Mortgage, Lehman Brothers, Bear Stearns, and AGI were also major customers posed a problematic conflict of interest. The Z-score, on the other hand, inherently avoids the bias and incestuous relationships demonstrated by many credit rating agencies during the run-up to the 2007–2008 crash.

The key takeaways of the Z-score formula for our purposes are the following: the use of different weights (e.g., EBIT or the C variable is more important than the Ratio of Working Capital / Total Assets or the A variable); a limited number of variables (more than two but fewer than six); and, leading (predictive) indicators. Mainly for informational purposes rather than applicability to the EWS proposed here, Altman's Z-score formula consists of the following five variables and weights:[2]

Z= (1.2) A + (1.4) B + (3.3) C + (0.6) D + E

A= Working Capital / Total Assets

B= Retained Earnings / Total Assets

C= Earnings Before Interest and Taxes / Total Assets

D= Market Value Equity / Total Liabilities

E= Sales / Total Assets

Creating a Z-Score Metric for Other Areas of Business

Can you create a universal Z-score type of formula to predict the likelihood of failure for new product introductions, company acquisitions, mergers, marketing, or sales campaigns? It's possible but highly unlikely for several reasons. Altman was able to create this universal score due to the availability of data from publicly traded companies that are required by law to provide a predetermined set of financial variables and do so on at least a quarterly and annual basis. Altman then compiled this data and compared companies that had gone bankrupt versus those that were successful. Through this process, he was able to use statistical analysis to identify key predictive variables (mainly ratios), assign differing weights to each, and arrive at a score that closely correlated with the likelihood of bankruptcy.

Unfortunately, there is no such publicly available data or standardized variables for products or campaigns that fail compared to those that are successful. Moreover, good luck trying to obtain detailed data from private or even public companies, especially when it comes to their failures. There are mathematical and simulation models available to predict product or market failure or underperformance. The purely mathematical models (static) are not widely used by industry because of their special data requirements, lack of customization, and accuracy rate of less than 70 percent. Market simulation software has a much better track record, with accuracy rates closer to 85 percent to 90 percent and are more customizable, but this type software is used primarily for major product introductions and in categories such as packaged goods (e.g., food products), consumer services (e.g., banking, travel), healthcare, and consumer durables (e.g., apparel, electronics). There must also be a substantial historical body of data on the category so that the simulation can be calibrated correctly for the initiative being forecasted. These types of software are also proprietary, so there is a cost associated with it, typically in the tens of thousands of dollar range, depending on the modules needed and complexity of the business or venture. Moreover, large companies often outsource customer acquisition campaigns to agencies; as a result, the campaign itself is not being monitored for failure or underperformance in real time. Therefore, although this software plays an important role in reducing failure in new product launches, it does not currently fulfill the role of an EWS, especially in the campaign area, because it focuses on lagging indicators and does not weigh or score the variances as an EWS should.

The main reason the Z-score is still widely used after 40 years by financial practitioners is its high accuracy rate and the fact that it can be calculated in minutes using a spreadsheet. Until that level of cost and simplicity is achieved, a one-size-fits-all tool will remain the domain of agencies and Fortune 500 companies and even then used mainly for forecasting new product introductions in certain categories and not as the EWS being proposed here.

An additional issue preventing the creation of a one-size-fits-all Z-score is that advertising, marketing, new product launches, and sales are incredibly heterogeneous. There are product extensions, launches in stable and low-competition environments versus those in volatile and high-competition industries, short versus long sales cycles, different stages in the life cycle, and so on. There is also a wide range of platforms available for your campaigns, such as radio, TV, PPC, social media, personal sales, and innumerable combinations of these, different levels of expenditures, and timeframes. Finally, every industry has its unique set of key drivers. Some are heavily impacted by commodity prices, others by repeat business, while others require ongoing customer acquisition and multiple combinations of these. In other words, the level of complexity and heterogeneity makes a simple and universal EWS nearly impossible.

Given the difficulty in creating some type of simple universal Z-score for products and especially for campaigns, a highly customizable and easy-to-build (using a spreadsheet) alternative is proposed and based on the same underlying principles as the Z-score.

The Option of Building a More Sophisticated EWS

Companies with the expertise and historical data can create a more sophisticated model that either builds on existing forecasting software or create their own from scratch. However, that level of complexity and cost is neither the focus nor the objective of this book. The focus here is on solutions for the "everyday manager and company." Domain transfers will never be widely adopted when cost and complexity are a significant factor.

In the final analysis, a sophisticated statistical EWS is still not a replacement for a causal forecast. Both approaches are actually complementary rather than mutually exclusive. The statistical model eliminates subjectivity and biases that a causal forecast may contain. However, the causal forecast has advantages not found in the statistical model, such as how it can be built it in a few hours in a spreadsheet; the thinking process that goes into building a causal forecast is as valuable as the EWS itself; and by having to list out the assumptions and key leading drivers, those responsible for the product or campaign are forced to be more in tune with the performance and effectiveness of the different platforms used and decisions made. An additional benefit of the causal over a sophisticated statistical model is that when something goes wrong, the business professional in charge can easily and instantly determine where the problem resides and proceed to fix it.

Case in point: If you were given a typical (non-causal) forecast predicting that a new B2B product launch would generate sales of 80 units per month during the first year, this forecast might not set off any alarm bells. However, if you were shown a causal forecast, in a few minutes you could see that it assumed a conversion rate of 35 percent, which might be four times higher than what your company had ever managed to achieve in the past.

Creating the EWS and Its Foundation, the Causal Forecast

The foundation for an EWS is to start by creating and fine-tuning a simple cause-and-effect type of forecasting method. There are many types of causal forecasts. Large companies use forecasting software that incorporates dozens of internal and external variables, including economic indicators such as changes in the cost of living, the unemployment rate, and so on. If you have the resources to leverage such a forecast to create an EWS, that's great, but fortunately, this is not necessary. All you need is a spreadsheet and a few hours to think through what initiatives generate revenue for your business. One driver is obviously repeat business, which might account for 40 percent of your revenues, but what about the rest? In the causal forecast, you detail all the different drivers that bring in customers, such as word of mouth, direct mail, digital campaigns, salespeople, and many more.

The casual forecast basically consists of assumptions, leading indicators (some are key revenue drivers, whereas others are foundations for success such as your distribution reach), "connector" variables, lagging indicators, and the extensive use of variance analysis between your actual results and forecasted goals. Figure 4.1 provides a high-level overview of the process for creating an EWS.

Step 1: The Assumptions

The assumptions are one of the most critical parts of both the causal forecast and EWS. Any business initiative, be it a financial investment, company acquisition, sales, marketing, or advertising effort, is based on certain underlying facts and evidence that drove the decision to pursue that particular initiative (e.g., launch a product or conduct a campaign). Very often, these assumptions are implicit, not detailed, and assumed to be true. For example, when proposing the acquisition of a company, we may make assumptions that are benign and probably factual while others lay the groundwork for failure. We might implicitly (perhaps correctly) assume, for example, that the economy will not go into a deep recession during the payback period, given that many economists and indicators show a healthy economic outlook for the next five years; or we may (incorrectly in this case) implicitly assume that the 12-month forecast provided by the seller is realistic, despite not having dissected the forecast and assumptions.

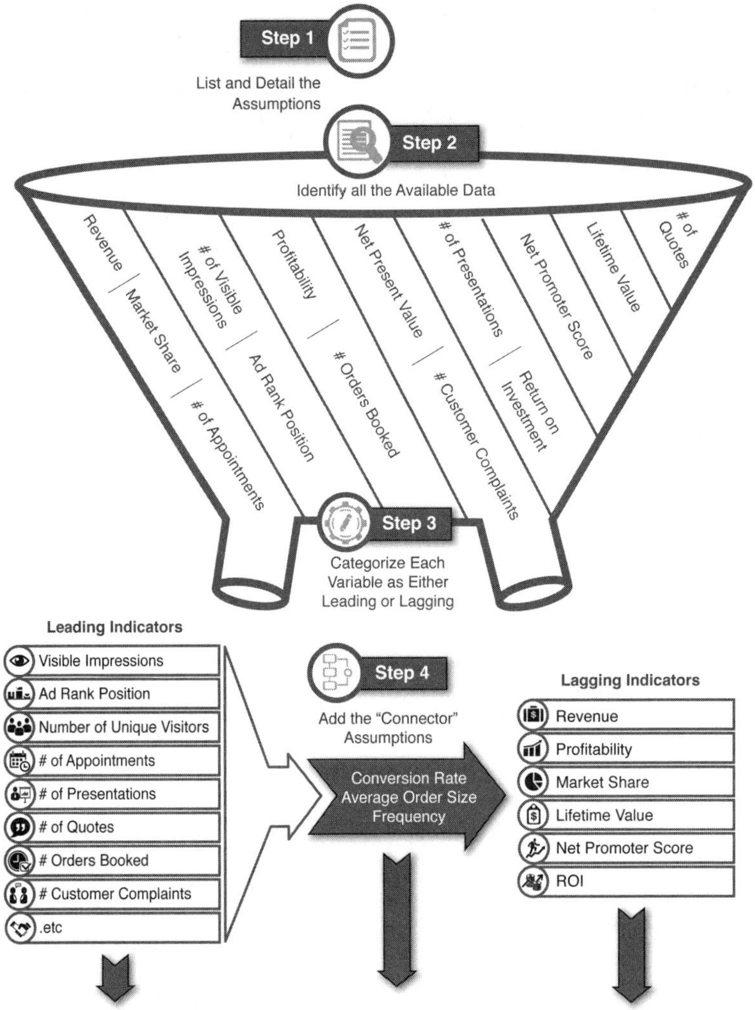

Figure 4.1 Overview of the creation of a causal forecast

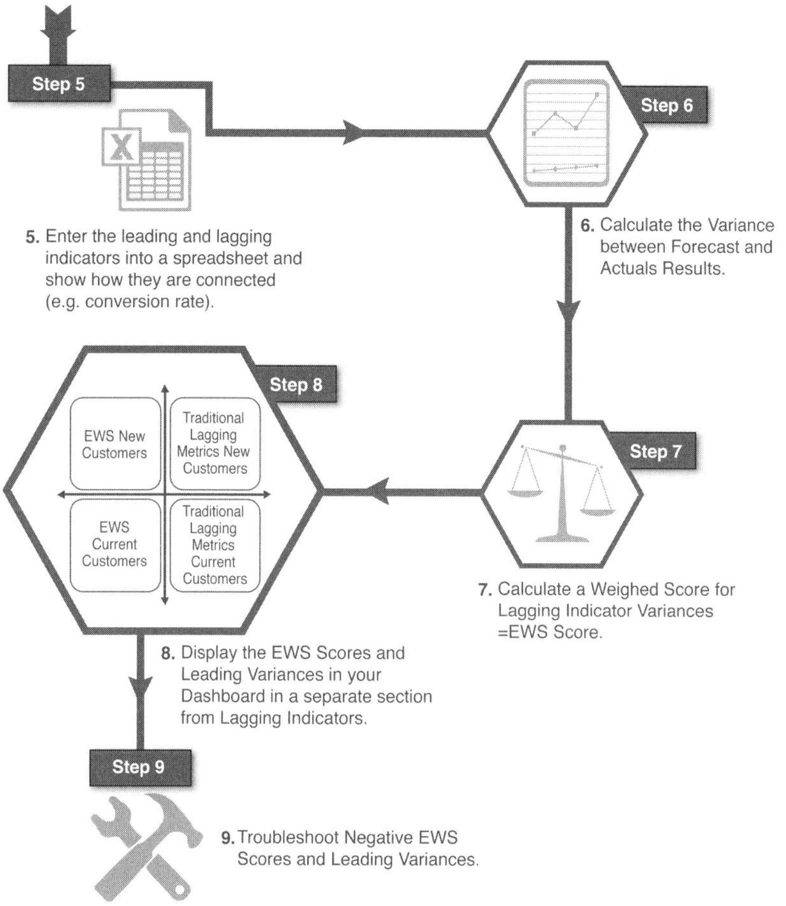

Figure 4.1 Continued

The assumptions should be the first part or section in any causal or other type of forecast and thus EWS. Assumptions require critical thinking and thoroughness because they can prevent serious blind spots and are important for troubleshooting purposes should your actual results deviate from your initial forecast. The list of assumptions should also include a detailed explanation of the basis upon which they are made and/or what evidence was used to make them. Table 4.1 shows an example of how to list and detail assumptions. Item 2, for example, states that the conversion rate is based on an industry benchmark. Any generic statement like this should be challenged to see how applicable it is to your particular situation.

Table 4.1 Example of Assumptions in a Causal Forecast

	Assumptions	What Evidence Is It Based On?
1	The conversion rate for unique number of visitors will be 8 percent if from organic traffic.	Web analytics data for previous 12 months.
2	The conversion rate for unique visitors that came from PPC display ads will be 3 percent.	Industry benchmark,* is used because a PPC campaign has never been done before, so there is no historical data available
3	The average order size from in-store orders will be $125 versus $75 for online orders.	Transactional data previous 12 months.
4	We are highly confident that our main competitor will not introduce a new product this year.	Vendor and client feedback received by our field sales representatives; in addition, our market research department has been monitoring the press and competitors' websites/social media.
5	We will have an awareness level of 30 percent prelaunch.	We are basing it on historical experience of different awareness levels based on a range of advertising reach and frequency (GRP).

* The Direct Marketing Institute offers a yearly "Response Rate Report" with success metrics for direct mail and digital platforms as well as their "Statistical Fact Book" with aggregated metrics from 70 leading companies.

Unfortunately, assumptions are often incorrectly estimated, based on "gut" feeling, and more often than not completely left out. An additional benefit of requiring this level of detail is that the manager responsible for the initiative will do a more thorough fact-checking job before sharing it with management. Finally, and if during a post-failure audit it is revealed how the fact checking was haphazard or an outright misrepresentation, that should be cause for corrective action, given that laziness or dishonesty are hard-to-fix root cause problems. For new products, the awareness level and distribution reach if applicable (Number of Outlets You Are In / Total Number of

Outlets Available for Your Category) should always be included in the assumptions section.

Leading Versus Lagging Indicators (The Foundation for Steps 2–4)

Lagging indicators (e.g., revenue) are those that follow an event(s), the result at the end of a given timeframe. Leading indicators (e.g., orders booked) are those that signal future outcomes and those that feed directly into the performance of an outcome (lagging). Performance management, economics, finance, digital, and direct marketing have all been using a combination of leading (forward-looking) and lagging (rear-looking) indicators for many years. Lagging indicators for economists are outcomes like the unemployment rate or a recession.

For economic leading indicators, one independent research association created *The Conference Board Leading Economic Index* for the United States, shown in Table 4.2.[3] As with the Z-score, each leading variable has been assigned a weight. However, given the complexity of an economy like ours, they used ten variables. This index has proven successful in predicting recessions, although it has given some false positives as well, predicting impending recessions that never materialized. In defense of this index, when the economy is starting to show signs of a recession, the Federal Reserve often starts taking actions that defer or prevent the forecasted recession.

Table 4.2 The Conference Board Leading Economic Index

Leading Variables Making Up the Index	Weights
1. Average weekly hours, manufacturing	0.2733
2. Average weekly initial claims for unemployment insurance	0.0328
3. Manufacturers' new orders, consumer goods and materials	0.0836
4. ISM Index of New Orders	0.1603
5. Manufacturers' new orders, nondefense capital goods excluding aircraft orders	0.0407

Leading Variables Making Up the Index	Weights
6. Building permits, new private housing units	0.0306
7. Stock prices, 500 common stocks	0.0394
8. Leading Credit Index	0.0829
9. Interest rate spread, 10-year Treasury bonds less federal funds	0.1108
10. Average consumer expectations for business conditions	0.1456
	1.0

Source: The Conference Board Leading Economic Index

One other type of indicator is called the *coincident.* It usually occurs at the same time as a leading or lagging indicator (e.g., "company profits" is a lagging indicator, and "average employee bonuses" would be a "coincident" indicator). When a company has sophisticated resources at its disposal, coincident indicators can be useful to pinpoint the dates when peaks or dips occur in the business cycle.

The EWS focuses mainly on leading indicators—which are the cornerstone of the EWS—and whose relevance must in turn be validated by lagging indicators and the "connector" assumptions that join the two types of indicators. For example, if you identified "orders booked" as a key leading indicator, this would need to be validated by a lagging indicator (e.g., revenue). However, what if "orders booked" was tracking the same as during a previous period and yet the company's revenue had actually declined? In this situation, there might be other leading indicators to better explain the decline, or you might have omitted other leading indicators, or perhaps made a faulty assumption in regards to the "average order size."

Step 2: Identifying All the Available Data

One approach to make sure that you do not leave anything out is to identify all the data variables you capture or could capture and then proceed to categorize and tag them as leading, lagging, or coincident, and then also as short term or long term. You may find that an increase in returns or complaints and a decline in unique website visitors are the earliest and leading indicators of the subsequent revenue decline. Chapter 5, "Blind Spots and Traps," provides some additional details on how to make sure that you are not missing out on relevant data points.

Step 3: Best Practices When Selecting and Categorizing Leading and Lagging Indicators

- **Short time frames:** Using monthly or quarterly data defeats the *raison d'être* of the EWS. Make sure that your causal forecast is broken down into daily or weekly time frames. Also resist the temptation to use averages. Instead, mimic any seasonal or day-of-the-week patterns your business exhibits. For example, if 70 percent of your orders occur on the weekend or during the last three months of the year, it would undermine the effectiveness of the EWS if you allocated them evenly throughout the weeks or months of the year.
- **Customers:** Separating new from existing customers is important because some of the leading indicators and connectors will be different. For example, in some companies, repeat business may account for 75 percent of annual revenues (e.g., a supermarket), whereas in other businesses (e.g., an appliance manufacturer), repeat customers may only account for 25 percent of annual revenues. Another benefit in separating new from existing customers is that it will save you time when troubleshooting a decline in performance and revenues.

- **Heterogeneity:** Because causal forecasts are incredibly heterogeneous, the leading indicators will be based on additional factors driven by your distribution model (online only versus a combination of brick-and-mortar and online versus indirect only through retailers), the average consumer decision-making purchase cycle (days, weeks, or months), and the stage in your product life cycle (as you move into each stage, you should adjust your leading indicators and assumption connectors).
- **Promotional drivers:** When creating a causal forecast, the primary but not exclusive focus is on "promotional" type leading indicators (e.g., ads, email, PPC, personal selling, *search engine optimization* [SEO], or catalogs) that generate revenue (lagging indicator). However, some leading indicators will not be promotional, such as awareness (do prospects even know your product or brand exists), distribution reach (e.g., in how many retailers is your product available), or on customer complaints. Table 4.3 provides some examples of both promotional and non-promotional leading indicators. Note that there are other non-promotional drivers such as price and distribution, but these will not be used when creating the EWS. Instead, they will be used for troubleshooting purposes if and when a variance occurs between your forecast and the actual results.
- **Special leading indicators:** Some leading indicators are either difficult or expensive to capture on an ongoing basis, such as awareness or brand recall. Short of large, statistically representative surveys or making assumptions based on the reach and frequency of your advertising (e.g., gross rating points), which is usually the domain of large companies, these types of leading indicators are not easy to track on a continuous basis. Table 4.3 shows a few examples of these special indicators.

Table 4.3 Examples of Different Types of Leading Indicators

Retail (Frozen Foods)	B2B (Cotton Gin Machinery)
New Customers	
Special non-promotional indicators:	**Special non-promotional indicators:**
Awareness level	Commodity prices for cotton (current and futures market)
Weather: temperatures	Volume of positive chatter on social media and news on cotton or alternative fabrics: fashion preferences (e.g., a new synthetic fabric)
Social media positive versus negative mentions and reviews	
Reach and display location	
Trends: GMO's, artificial ingredients (can be tracked with social media platforms and market research)	
Promotional:	**Promotional:**
Promotions targeted to noncustomers, coupons	Number of appointments with prospects
Promotions to the distributor	Number of quotes generated
TV advertising	Number of orders booked
Current Customers	
Special non-promotional indicators:	**Special non-promotional indicators:**
Brand recall	Commodity price for cotton (current and futures)
Weather	Trend with repeat business rates
Number of customer complaints	Increase in planted cotton acreage
Social media positive versus negative mentions	Stage in the lifecycle of current equipment
Reach and display position	Number of complaints and returns for machinery or parts
Change in ingredients/taste	
Promotional:	**Promotional:**
Promotions to customers: Coupons	Number of contacts per year with customers
Promotions to the distributor	Number of inquiries from customers
TV advertising (gross rating points)	Number of quotes generated
	Number of orders booked

- **Using social media listening platforms to capture leading indicator sentiment:** For some of these difficult-to-quantify leading indicators, some businesses with a strong digital customer engagement level might be able to aggregate several variables using a social media analytics platform to come up with a plausible "awareness index" (Volume of Product Mentions / Total Category Mentions, along with some positive versus negative sentiment weighing). Another option is to consider using the keyword search term query volume tools provided by Google and Bing, which you can then use to compare to brands in your category (e.g., if the three top brands in the category have a combined total of 100,000 monthly searches and Brand A has 20%, Brand B 50%, and Brand C 30%, this can be used as a rough indicator of consumer preference). A cautionary note if using a social media listening platform: Many conversations are private (e.g., many Facebook posts), so make sure that any heavily weighted source such as Twitter (which usually has the largest volume of publicly available data that these tools are allowed to access) is a statistically valid representation of your target market. If not, you could be making assumptions based on Twitter mentions by users who might represent less than 2 percent of your target market.

Example of a Social Media Analytics Platform Used to Capture a Leading Indicator

Figure 4.2 shows how Schick had a significant increase in Facebook fans during a certain period; additional research revealed that Schick was giving away product by bundling it with other online product offers through a partnership with key online retailers and a sports website. So while the increase in Schick Facebook fans was modest compared with Gillette's base, this could act as a leading competitive indicator that could interfere with Gillette's promotional campaign. The social media listening platform may also capture customer complaints and reveal that your sampling campaign is not performing as expected.

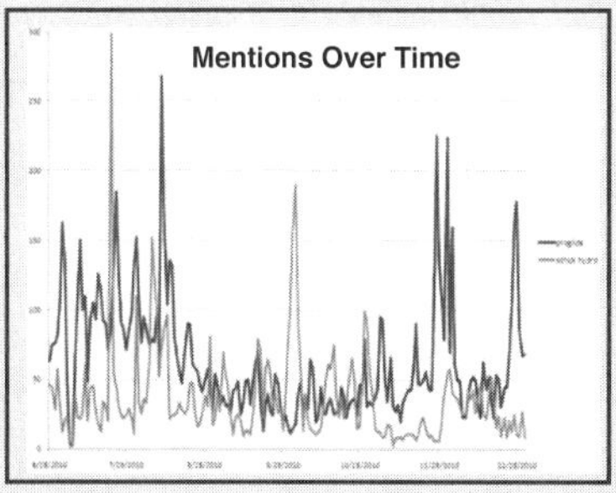

Gillette	Schick Hydro Experience
fans (start) 304,766	fans (start) 29,378
fans (end) 305,766	fans (end) 63,309
change **+1,000**	change **+33,931**

"Pretty disappointed with Gillette. I've been a loyal customer yet I have not received the free ProGlide sample. My uncle received his and we both had sent our submissions in at the same time (both of which went through, and it said I'd receive it in 8-9ish days)."

Figure 4.2 Example of a social media analytics platform and leading indicators (Source: MutualMind)

Lagging indicators are the easiest to identify. These are the outcomes through which your company defines success. Examples are metrics such as the number of orders, revenue, profitability, market share, return on investment, lifetime value, net promoter score, and so on. The most important consideration when selecting the lagging indicators is to make sure that you have picked the leading indicators that are best translating and driving your lagging indicator.

Insight

For companies that sell directly and only online, the lines between leading and lagging indicators may be blurred, given that a sale may occur on the same day as the leading indicator (unique visitors and the order). However, with additional brainstorming and research, you can find other leading indicators. Perhaps a downward trend in your website's organic search page rank for high-converting keywords or average PPC ad rank position can presage future declines in website traffic and orders.

Step 4: Adding the "Connector" Assumptions

Connectors are those values, often expressed as percentages, that translate promotional leading indicators into lagging indicators as shown in Table 4.4. These connector variables can encompass a wide range of variables but are usually metrics such as click-through rates, conversion rates, average order sizes, repeat purchase rate, and so on.

Table 4.4 Example of Leading, Connector, and Lagging Variables

Leading: Promotional driver	Forecast	Connector: Conversion rate forecasted	Lagging: New customer orders forecasted
Number of fliers mailed	2,000	2.5%	50

Step 5: Entering Leading, Lagging, and Connectors into a Spreadsheet

The next steps are all outlined in greater detail in the Appendix with a sample spreadsheet in Table A.1, that shows where the leading, connector, and lagging indicators are entered and also where, for each indicator and connector assumption, "actual" numbers are entered next to the forecasted values.

Step 6: Calculating the Variance

The "actuals" are the results (numbers) that come in after you complete your different campaign initiatives. Most variance calculations are pretty straightforward (e.g., the [Actual results-Forecasted results]/ Forecasted results) as the example in Table 4.5 shows. Moreover, when the "actuals" are greater than the forecasted amount, that is usually a good thing, and you have beat your forecast. However, there are a few situations or cases where you are tracking a ranking (where ad position 1 is better than position 3); how to deal with these cases is explained in the Appendix, in Table A.2.

Table 4.5 Example of a Typical Variance Calculation

Leading: Promotional driver	Forecasted new customer orders	Actual new customer orders	Variance in the number of new customer orders
Number of fliers mailed	50	18	–32 (–64%)

Step 7: Calculating a Weighed Scored

This step requires calculating weights for the lagging indicator so that you can prioritize your early warning system. Table A.1 in the Appendix shows how the weights are calculated (the number of new customer orders forecasted for a given initiative divided by the total number of orders forecasted). Each driver will have its own individually weighted score, which can be negative or positive; with a cumulative score for all the lagging indicators. The objective of the weighed score is so that you can focus on the higher negative values in your EWS to see what needs to be prioritized.

Step 8: The EWS Dashboard

Table 4.6 shows what the EWS section of your business dashboard might look like. These measures are all entirely customizable, with some companies perhaps wanting to show only negative variances to reduce the clutter. Details of how these numbers were obtained are explained in more detail in the Appendix in Table A.1.

Table 4.6 EWS Dashboard

EWS	Variance			
Assumptions				
Average ad rank position PPC	–47%			
Organic search page average rank for top five converting keywords	–60%			
Awareness index (= Positive Mentions / Total Category Mentions)	233%			
Distribution (= # Outlets In / Total # of Outlets)	–29%			
Number of complaints per week	25%			
Promotional leading drivers	**Variance Leading Indicators**	**Variance Conversion Rate**	**Variance New Customer Orders**	**EWS Weighed Variance Score***
Organic web traffic—from blog, YouTube, Twitter, Instagram, and SEO: unique visitors	–8%	–15%	–22	**–6.6**
Web traffic from affiliates: unique visitors	6%	20%	0	**0.00**
PPC (visible impressions)	6%	–28%	–30	**–11.1**
Number of on-hold messages with partner companies	–30%	–27%	–1	**–0.01**
Number of mail-order catalogs mailed	–7%	7%	0	**0**
Number of people attending PR events	7%	–27%	–10	**–1.3**
Number of fliers mailed	–10%	–60%	–32	**–4.8**
Totals			**–95**	**–24**

* Based on new orders forecasted for that initiative as a percentage of total forecasted orders-see Table A.1 in the Appendix

Step 9: Troubleshooting: When the EWS Shows Underperformance

When multiple negative variances appear, focus on the higher EWS scores because those are the ones that will impact the lagging indicators (e.g., revenue) the most. In Table 4.7, we are only highlighting two important negative indicators for the sake of brevity. Without running a regression, there is probably some correlation between some of the assumptions and the negative outcomes. For example, the decline in "average ad rank position" is probably a contributor to the negative leading indicator "PPC" and its poor conversion rate. When an ad rank drops (it becomes less visible to most prospects), you can safely assume based on experience and historical data that the click-through rate and conversion rate will also decrease. The Appendix shows a detailed troubleshooting tree in Table A.5.

Table 4.7 Negative Variances for Troubleshooting

Promotional Leading Drivers	Variance Leading Indicators	Variance Conversion Rate	Variance New Customer Orders	EWS Weighed Variance
PPC-visible impressions based on average 1.5 ad rank	6%	–28%	–30	–11.12
Number of fliers mailed	–10%	–60%	–32	–4.81

Because the EWS provides such granular detail of where the problem resides, conducting a *root cause analysis* (RCA) will take a lot less time now. In this example, for the PPC negative variance, the drop in ad rank position could be due to many causes, some of which would be easy to identify (e.g., a lower-than-suggested bid), whereas others may be less obvious (e.g., poor quality of the written ads).

Once you find a failure cause, look back at your controls and detection measures in the FMEA for this initiative and add or tighten any preventive control or detection measures.

The EWS is both a learning and preventive tool. The learning component resides in that it helps business owners or managers carefully think through their key revenue and other leading indicator drivers. These are usually not broken down and evaluated in any systematic manner by managers. Only good things can happen when the manager has a good pulse on what is and isn't working and what drivers matter the most. The preventive component of the EWS is more obvious because it alerts early on about the underperformance so that prompt corrective action can be taken. The benefits are no different than with the early detection of diseases or conditions like diabetes or high blood pressure versus finding out you have them while at the emergency room.

5

Blind Spots and Traps

"The fault, dear Brutus, is not in our stars, but in ourselves."

—William Shakespeare, *Julius Caesar*

Thus far, the cold hard statistics of failure and underperformance have been analyzed, and better decision-making frameworks have been discussed. You've learned how to failure-proof major initiatives through a *failure mode and effects analysis* (FMEA), how to get to the underlying cause of a failure through *root cause analysis* (RCA), and also how to create an *early warning system* (EWS). In this chapter, the focus is on common business blind spots and traps that account for a significant percentage of failure and underperformance. Peter Drucker, considered the father of modern management consulting, stated that business had only two functions—marketing and innovation—with all other functions playing supporting roles. I, too, focus on these key areas, along with the research and decision making that drives those and many other areas.

As described in the first chapter, numerous studies and articles over time have compiled a lengthy laundry list of reasons why business and product failures occur. It includes everything from strategic to financial reasons such as negative cash flow. However, these are usually proximate or immediate causes of failure and underperformance rather than underlying root causes. Since every business is different, there is *no* substitute for conducting your own FMEA and failure audit using RCA. While keeping that in mind, this chapter is designed to serve as a collection of common underlying problems with some cases and evidence so that companies and individuals can get a feel for the types of common root causes they may encounter. It would be pretentious to portray this as a comprehensive listing of all the underlying causes of failure. In fact, one ongoing project is a request that readers share and suggest by functional area (e.g., HR, finance) common failure problems and case study examples at my blog: www.breakingfailure.com. The objective is to eventually update this chapter with functional area-specific sections. Because the solutions covered in this section are not a domain transfer per se, there is an element of subjectivity, but hopefully grounded in common sense, relevant case studies, and evidence.

Areas of Failure: Knowns and Unknowns

"Unforeseen" events and their often negative consequences-at least for some of those involved-occur in every area of life, including politics (Obama beating Hillary Clinton in the primaries), war (Iraq and its aftermath), the economy (mortgage implosion in 2008), transportation (NASA Challenger disaster), medicine (discovery that hormone replacement therapy used for decades created a significant risk of cancer), and in the personal realm (divorce). The problem is not just that they happen, but that if pointed out as a possible outcome early on, the observation is usually dismissed as highly improbable, if not impossible

During the Iraq war, and in an exasperated attempt to justify the many missteps, then-Secretary of Defense Rumsfeld, if nothing else, explained the issue well. Rumsfeld stated that there are the "known-knowns" or things we know that we know (e.g., we are launching a new product next month), others that are "known-unknowns" or things we know we do not know (e.g., the exact number of units we will sell), and finally there are the "unknown-unknowns," those events we don't know we don't know (e.g., a future disruptive technology). The problem with Rumsfeld's self-serving analysis, or Wall Street's (post-2008 recession) excuses for that matter, is that they attributed their fiascos to the unknowns, despite the fact that several reputable people had brought up the high probability of a negative and far different outcome than what the public or markets were being told. Far left philosopher-critic Slavoj Žižek sarcastically added a fourth scenario regarding Rumsfeld, which he called the "unknown-known," or that which we *intentionally* refuse to acknowledge we know.[1]

Let's look at each of these situations, given that they all contribute to problems and how to identify, mitigate, or prevent their occurrence. A summary of the areas and problems to be covered is provided in Figure 5.1.

The "Known-Knowns"

Most professionals believe this area is straightforward and under control, when in fact it's a source of a majority of problems. Leaving aside those cases when business professionals don't even bother with research, important decisions are usually based on market research and data analytics. However, the data used to justify the recommendations is seldom verified for accuracy or to ensure there are no gaps. A valid argument is that one has to trust the researcher or analyst, otherwise not much work would get done. However, until that person or department has implemented a FMEA and RCA program to identify gaps or root causes of failure, "business as usual" will continue to produce high failure and underperformance rates.

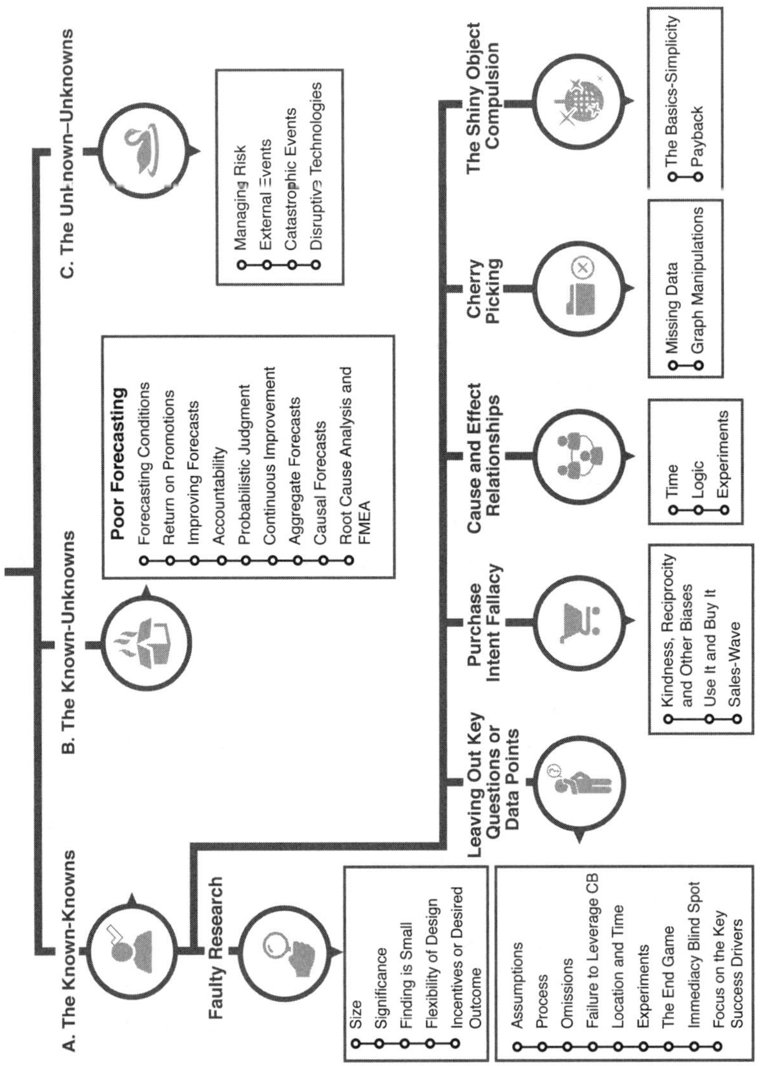

Figure 5.1 Overview of frequent causes of failure

Problem 1: Faulty Research

> *"Research is what I'm doing when I don't know what I'm doing."*
>
> —Werner von Braun, German rocket scientist

Despite numerous articles and books warning against relying on small samples for research or experiments, many professionals continue to misuse them, abandoning their qualitative and exploratory nature and extrapolating the findings to the larger target market. Social media analytics can also have the same unrepresentative sampling problems present in focus groups. There is a natural self-selection bias at work in social media. In some cases, it might be representative of the target population. However, is the opinion of heavy Facebook users, who might represent less than 10 percent of your target market, something to hang your hat on? In the case of traditional focus groups, in addition to not being representative, they suffer from many other sins, including the potential for group think. A study published in the magazine *Marketing Research* of more than 673 focus group participants also revealed how over half said money was their primary motivation for being involved.[2]

In 2005, an academic paper titled "Why Most Published Research Findings Are False," by Dr. John Ioannidis, an epidemiologist at Stanford, sent shockwaves through the medical academic research community, receiving in the process over 1,300 citations. (The average number of citations varies by discipline, but most academic papers receive fewer than 20 citations.)[3] To this day, and despite the controversy, Ioannidis's findings have not been disproven. The only serious criticism was that the title was scandalous, given that many researchers know this can be a problem. This might be true, but there are no such disclaimers attached to the research.

One reason for this problem is the over interpretation of statistical significance in studies. Often you will hear the mention of *p-value* as evidence that the study demonstrated a statistically significantly difference (despite being done with a small sample size). Anti-Bayesian British statistician Sir Ronald Fisher adopted a method by which the p-value of .05 became a reference point for how confident one should be of a research finding. The p-value is the probability that there might be data significantly different from what was observed in a given experiment. A p-value of .05 means that there is only a 5 percent chance that there might be data considerably more extreme or different than the data observed in the finding.

However, this widely accepted threshold is considered insufficient by a growing number of researchers. Texas A&M University professor Dr. Valen Johnson, writing in the prestigious journal *Proceedings of the National Academy of Sciences,* argued that a p-value of .05 is far too weak a standard. Johnson says that the probability of seeing more extreme data is not the same as the probability that the tested hypothesis is true. In fact, Johnson states that when using a p-value of .05, there is actually still a 20 percent to 25 percent chance that the reported findings aren't true. This problem is more prevalent in biology, the social sciences, and health fields and in part is driven by the difficulty in easily obtaining large sample sizes. For business professionals in those fields and who are relying on experimental research to make important business decisions, this should be a cautionary note. The .05 p-value is also appearing in studies and experiments in social media, so this can be an issue in any business using small sample sizes and p-values of .05. In physics, for example, the p-value threshold has been tightened considerably to 0.0000003 as in the case of the Higgs Boson discovery.[4]

The continued use of the .05 standard is due in great measure to how it greatly facilitates being able to pick up some effect even in a smaller-sized experiment, something that would rarely be attainable with a more stringent level of .01. The problem with a p-value of .05 is that many of these findings cannot later be replicated or validated, thereby effectively making them misleading. Ioannidis's and Johnson's concerns have been validated repeatedly by industry. For example, Bayer (Amgen Pharmaceutical had similar findings) published a study describing how it had to halt nearly two-thirds of its early drug target projects because in-house experiments failed to match the claims made in the literature.[5]

Solution: Ioannidis and Johnson's findings can be repurposed into our business context as errors that should be avoided. Therefore, studies are less likely to be true in the following scenarios:

- A small or potentially unrepresentative sample is used (e.g., focus groups, social media).
- The statistical threshold for a study or experiment being true is at the .05 or 5 percent level.
- The difference or finding is small (e.g., concept X has 3 percent more customer preference than concept Y).
- The research design is flexible (e.g., no actual use of the product by those surveyed).
- There is an incentive for a specific outcome desired by the researcher/management (e.g., monetary or for career progression).

Business professionals should thus follow up any small-scale research, models, or experiments with larger sample or data sets and set a higher statistical threshold p-value of at least .01 when using small sample sizes. Moreover, if data sets are used and a correlation is found, determine whether there is a cause-effect relationship or, if two effects, identify the underlying cause. This issue on cause and effects will be covered in problem 4. With his Greek surname, Ioannidis's warnings should be known as the "Ioannidis Prophesy."

Problem 2: Leaving Out Key Questions or Data Points

"Facts do not cease to exist because they are ignored."

—Aldous Huxley, *Complete Essays*

Often, you may have a desired outcome in mind and expect the research to confirm the hunch. As a result, discomforting questions or data are prone to being left out. This dangerous inclination is known as the *confirmation bias,* whereby a person reaches a conclusion *a priori* and then proceeds to seek out, highlight, and include data that upholds his beliefs while disregarding as an outlier or coincidence anything that contradicts the desired outcome. This is what Slavoj Žižek was referring to with his concept of the "unknown-known" or denial of facts. Nassim Taleb illustrated this blind spot with the story of a turkey who, in the weeks leading up to Thanksgiving, was being well fed by the farmer. The turkey's hypothesis that the farmer had his best interests in mind was confirmed day after day, until Thanksgiving rolled around. Unfortunately, the turkey left out a key data point, which was what had occurred to previous turkeys on that date.

Numerous failures have resulted from this type of bias or error whereby critical information was either not collected or not included in the market research conclusions. This occurred to Motorola in 1991 when it launched Iridium, a spin-off, to pursue a global satellite networks for consumer mobile usage. To justify that decision, Motorola conducted one of the largest market research efforts ever seen, screening 200,000 candidates and selecting 23,000 individuals in 42 countries and 3,000 corporations for interviews. Using a small sample was clearly not the issue. By all accounts, they used correct sampling methodologies for the selection and sample size determination.

According to Motorola, the research findings overwhelmingly supported going forward with the launch. The exact percentages are unknown, but many of the recommendations were based on purchase intent questions (more on this shortly). We do know that important details were not shared with the respondents, such as the phone, costing an average of $3,000, was the size of a brick and could not be used in moving cars or inside buildings. Moreover, the overwhelming majority of respondents never got to try out the phones. Their responses were solely based on hypothetical scenarios. When the service was finally launched in 1998 (a lot of technological changes had also occurred since the start of the project), Iridium enrolled fewer than 20,000 subscribers during the first year versus the 600,000 forecasted. Iridium declared bankruptcy that same year, losing at least $2.5 billion in addition to countless lawsuits from investors and creditors over the following years. While the causes for the failure were many, this omission error laid the foundation for their unachievable projection of 600,000 units in year one.[6]

Another case in which the "knowns" were assumed to be correct occurred with the New Coke introduction back in the 1980s. In this instance, Coke was provoked by the successful "Pepsi Challenge" campaign in the 1970s, where televised, on-the-street, blind taste tests showed that consumers preferred Pepsi over Coke and which contributed to Pepsi's market share growing from 20 percent in 1970 to 28 percent by 1980. Coke conducted their own blind taste tests that, much to their dismay, validated Pepsi's findings. After many months of frenetic research, their R&D department came up with a formula that in blind taste tests beat both the old Coke and Pepsi. Coke invested approximately $4 million in their blind taste tests, which included some 191,000 people in 13 cities, 55 percent of whom preferred the new formula over Coke and Pepsi.[7]

With a great deal of fanfare, Coke announced to the world the "New Coke" product and retired the old Coke. However, Coke soon faced a firestorm of protests and complaints from apoplectic loyal customers. If this had happened in today's social media world, Facebook and Twitter's websites would have probably crashed. After several weeks of damage control, Coca-Cola decided to bring back the Old Coke, hence known as Coca-Cola Classic, while keeping the newborn as New Coke (Coke II) until it was eventually dropped altogether around 2002.

What went wrong? The market research was done correctly from a sampling and methodological standpoint. The problem was what was *not* included in the research. All the taste tests were "blind." However, when non-blind taste tests were conducted during a postmortem and consumers shown which brand they were drinking, opinions changed dramatically, with Coke being preferred over Pepsi and the New Coke by a wide margin. Why were blind taste tests not representative? Because consumer preferences are not just about taste; they are about emotions, childhood memories, and brand loyalty for an iconic product. As a footnote, when during the prelaunch a few focus group participants were told that the new formulation would be called Coke, there were some negative comments, but this was never followed-up on, and that's a clear case of ignoring discomforting data. There were other factors that have been mentioned, such as the fact that in the case of some small sips, a sweeter taste would probably win, but all those factors are encompassed by the fact that in a non-blind taste, they simply do not matter.

Solution: Usually the research proposal or final report will list the objectives, methodology, key findings, and recommendations. However, for important projects, managers should review and request the inclusion of certain key information. Here are some of the major areas that should be included:

- **Assumptions:** Chapter 4, "The Early Warning System," focused on assumptions that should be included along with the forecast. However, assumptions should be included not just with forecasts but with any major business recommendation. Consider a recommendation for a new product add-on, based on the assumption that the data used only current customers when in reality the data contained a large percentage of customers that had been inactive for five years. Would you want to roll out a product add-on based on that data? Once assumptions are listed, require that details be provided regarding the source or basis upon which they were made. The assumptions could also be prioritized in terms of the potential impact if they differ from the prediction or assumption (e.g., the interest rate will remain below 5 percent). The final step is to verify and validate that those assumptions are in fact correct, that the appropriate date ranges were selected, and that the definitions are specific (e.g., is a current customer one who bought something in the past 18, 24, or 36 months?)

Areas that should be included in the assumptions section include the following:

— What baseline projections were used (e.g., growth rates, units sold)?

— What is the predicted competitive response or action (e.g., they will not launch a new product)?

— What change if any is being assumed for the following key factors: advertising, distribution, costs, legislation, the economy, and so on. If a change is expected, that should be detailed (e.g., we will have additional distribution in 500 stores in the southeast region).

— An assessment, if the research includes testing or sampling, on what is different from a real-world situation (e.g., no one buys a soft drink by blind tasting it).

- **Established processes:** As discussed in Chapter 3, "The Business Failure Audit and the Domain Transfer of Root Cause Analysis," having a well-defined process and enforcing it through the use of mandatory checklists is critical to avoid missing a step or action item. Checklists, however, can create a false sense of security if you believe they are comprehensive and static. Inevitably, and especially when being used for the first time, something will be left out. A good example occurs in financial auditing, which uses all kinds of benchmarks and ratios (e.g., itemized deductions/income). Exceed them and you're likely to be audited. Unfortunately, those who so desire often use creative tricks to stay out of the "check-listed" audit items—Enron, for example, used multiple "raptor" companies to hide liabilities and a convoluted "mark to market" system for asset and liability valuations.[8] Failure is that way as well; it somehow seems to always find the "loopholes." To avoid this problem, use a FMEA, and if you already do and a failure occurs, conduct an RCA to make sure that you are not leaving anything out of the checklist. Any omissions or weaknesses should be added to the control and detection mechanisms listed in the FMEA.

- **Data omissions:** As in boxing, it's usually the punch you did not see coming that knocks you out, which is why preventive measures such as proper defensive hand, foot, body, and eye positions are the best safeguards. In business, the best preventive measures are the use of a well-documented process, mandatory checklists, a FMEA, and an RCA. One technique to prevent omissions involves the following three-step process:

1. First, list all the areas or data points being used in the analysis or research.
2. Then compare them against all the data your company currently gathers in the course of business and identify data not currently included in your analysis or research. Often, a company has different databases and collects scores or hundreds of variables but uses less than a dozen on a regular basis. Look at the data not included and decide whether any of it should be included; in many cases, you may not want to include data because it may create what is called *noise* (irrelevant data points that obfuscate the important ones).
3. The final step is to identify relevant data not being collected. This requires time, thought, and effort. One method is to create a storyboard of a consumer as they go through the purchase decision process, as shown in Figure 5.2. As you go through this process, identify what additional pieces of data might be beneficial for your analysis to better predict behaviors and outcomes in any of these key stages.

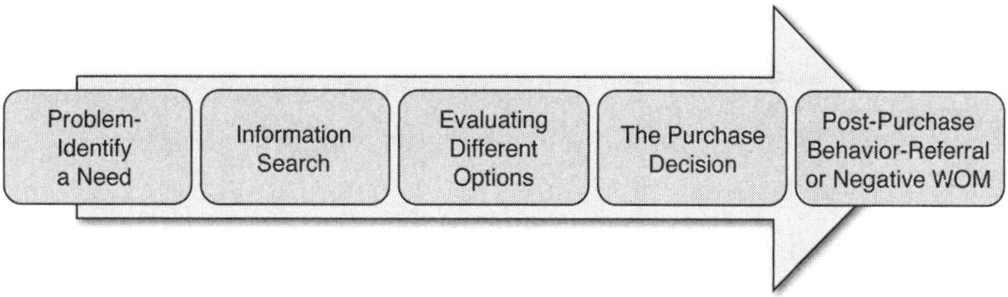

Figure 5.2 Consumer decision-making process

For example, if McDonald's wants to target "stay at home" moms for lunch, researchers may fall for the *availability bias*, looking only at the data they currently have. Suppose they have a social media listening platform that collects blog, Twitter, and Facebook data. The fact that the information collected may be voluminous often creates the perception that this is all they need. Of course, you should analyze the data you have, but (and if you want to avoid surveys) also look at key areas of the process such as the "information search" aspect of this decision-making process. Determine what other sources of information mothers might look at aside from the ones you are collecting. Perhaps through brainstorming or other research, you realize that rating and review sites may contain valuable insights. In fact, most if not all major social media analytics platforms currently do not capture review sites like Yelp, which is a major blind spot. This insight might uncover the fact that cleanliness is a key attribute moms consider when determining which fast food restaurant to go to for a lunch outing. With this new insight, perhaps city restaurant health inspection ratings along with review sites might be valuable variables to start including when determining store-level performance, as shown in Figure 5.3. In addition, this insight allows McDonald's to pay attention and notify those restaurants locations with low or mediocre health scores.

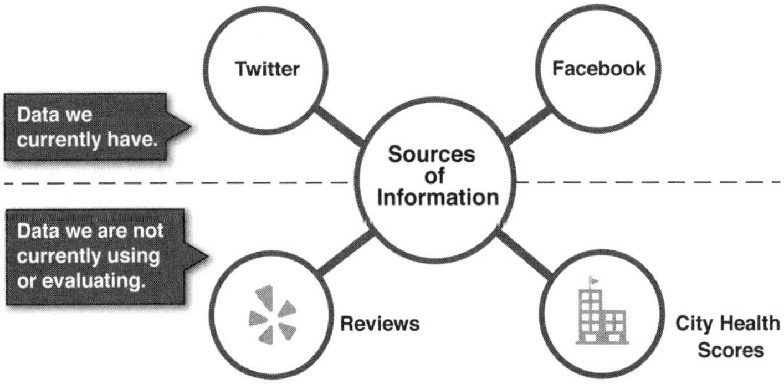

Figure 5.3 Example of Identifying Missing Data

> Another way to identify data that can help solve a problem is to conduct other types of research such as observational research to try to determine which other data points might be missing. For example, if you cannot explain why on some days your sales are down during peak times, visit the store. You may discover there aren't enough cashiers during these periods. As a result, some customers buy fewer items so that they can use the express checkout, while others leave without buying anything. With this finding, it would make sense to include the number of cashiers on duty on any given day and time as a variable. If you only looked at the data collected, you might have attributed the cause incorrectly to the coincidental opening of a competitor's store a few miles away and lowered your prices.

Often we have to look at the trees for the forest and vice versa:

- **The forest:** Macro data can be highly beneficial in helping connect the dots, since with "big data," it is easy to get lost in the details. Always see whether macro-level data can be included or created by aggregating existing micro-level data. For example, while the day/time provides useful information, an additional field representing the season provides a broader context (e.g., summer is when kids are out of school), which can help trigger connections and insights from the analyst. Another example: Web analytics is usually looked at on a platform-by-platform basis (e.g., the company website, Facebook) but not aggregated into one, which if done properly could highlight a trend not otherwise easily visible when the traffic volume for each individual platform is not enough to pick up on that trend or issue.

- **The tree:** Sometimes it's the opposite that's needed, further breaking down or collecting more detailed variables. Recently, I visited a big box retailer, Garden Ridge, which sells crafts and home decor. These 100,000 square-foot stores sell (mainly on the value side) everything from furniture and paintings to kitchenware and Christmas decorations. I observed that at least 25 percent to 30 percent of the furniture and a larger percentage of the artwork had chips, scratches, or some other damage. While it is true that this is in part due to the lower quality of the products, if packaged and handled better at least the cheapness wouldn't be as evident. Unless the store is capturing the specific reason and details of a markdown (e.g., the type of damage—scratches versus chips—by product category or *stock-keeping unit* [SKU]), the store might be blaming the markdown on the wrong cause.

  However, in this example, simply identifying that a large percentage of merchandise is damaged is not enough. An RCA should be done to determine the underlying cause: Is it the vendor shipping damaged merchandise? Is the carrier mishandling it, or are the store employees doing the damage when they are putting it out on the floor? Or are the customers mishandling the merchandise on display? Perhaps it is some combination of these. Identifying the type of damage by SKU/vendor would go a long way toward remedying the situation. Effective remedial action is often not possible unless the root cause has been identified.

- **Failure to leverage consumer behavior with analytics:** Many analytics departments are staffed by economists, programmers, and statisticians who are often uninformed about consumer behavior principles, leaving potentially valuable insights off the table, as was seen in the McDonald's example. Those tasked with insight development often fail to reference these elements and therefore the possible impact that their recommendations may have on other key elements in the customer relationship.

  For example, many airlines have crunched the numbers and to make some additional revenue added an extra row or two of seats to their airplanes, reducing leg space in the process. However, on a few occasions, this has led to fights between passengers serious enough to make the plane divert course and land at the nearest airport. Is the incremental revenue from the extra row of seats compensating for the cost of a flight diversion? Even in less-extreme situations, are those cost savings worth the stress and passenger ill-will being created? The thought of going through long security lines and then being herded into a high-priced flying Greyhound bus with no food is not very appealing.

  Therein lies the trap. The airlines have unwittingly introduced into a traveler's consideration set an alternative option that did not previously exist. Travelers may now consider driving instead of flying, even for a five- to eight-hour car trip, whereas perhaps the driving option was only previously considered if less than a five-hour drive.

- **Include location and time data:** This data is becoming more commonplace thanks to mobile devices. Its importance cannot be overstated, and probably some of the best insights will come from mobile data. Consider the scenario where Frank clicked on a video ad on Tuesday. With mobile geo-location data, there is now the ability to know the rest of the story: That he walked into a Tesla dealership on Friday at 6 p.m., and thanks to the *Internet of Things* (IoT), that he drove out with a Tesla two hours later, doing 70 mph in a 55 mph zone, triggering an increase in his auto insurance premium. One potentially IoT blockbuster opportunity for consumer durable goods manufacturers is the ability to target consumers when a product is reaching the end of its life cycle, or if the appliance malfunctions it could be remotely diagnosed, triggering a repair quote or scheduling one if under warranty.

With the advent of proximity "ibeacons" and mobile payments, encouraging customers to use mobile coupon or loyalty store apps will open a treasure trove of in-store behavioral data. Today, retailers know the revenue per square foot for each department. Tomorrow, retailers will be able to add metrics such as browsing time per square foot and compare that against conversions per square foot by category or department. Sound like web analytics? You bet it does. We may reach a point when brick-and-mortar stores will have the ability to use web analytic-type metrics such as bounce rates, "walk-through" paths, time in store, and many more.

Moreover, data management platforms such as IBM's Lotane or Oracle's BlueKai collect not just *customer relationship management* (CRM) and campaign data (*pay per click* [PPC], email, etc.), but also offline data (real estate, car ownership, etc.). As store geo-proximity data becomes more widely available and analysis capacity improves, true omni-channel capabilities and insights will finally be achieved. In fact, we may eventually adopt one set of standardized metrics for both online and offline shopping, leveraging insights that were previously only available with online shopping. For example, perhaps those customers who browse through the handbag section of the store for more than three minutes are 80 percent more likely to buy from the shoe department. This information could lead to improved and optimized planograms and store layouts, as is done with websites that are driven by web analytics data. Given privacy laws and concerns, this tracking data will be available only to merchants through opt-in programs, which is why mobile loyalty and discount programs will play an ever-larger role.

- **The omission of experiments and testing:** The temptation to "go big or go home" is a frequent trap. This usually implies bypassing a test or a slow ramp-up (on a smaller scale initially). As discussed in Chapter 1, "Failure & Stagnation," the *action bias* is frequently at work among business professionals and especially with entrepreneurs. The opportunity seems too good to start out slow or do a test. Under some conditions, this might be true. In the book's Introduction, I mentioned the truism that "volume hides a multitude of sins." Large companies can indulge in this type of risk taking because if the potential downside is kept to a small percentage of their overall revenues, the damage will be inconsequential. Google is a perfect example. Many think of them as a "new product success machine," but that is very far from the truth. Google has shut down many initiatives and ventures, including Google Checkout, Notebook, Page Creator, Audio Ads (radio), and Buzz, while keeping others on life support, such as Google Plus.

  Bypassing testing or a slow ramp-up might be a valid option if and when the following conditions are met:

— Accelerating the time to market is demonstrably critical, especially if the competition is either likely to or is already ramping up to enter (i.e., a competitor is undergoing extensive testing and has a jump start on you for that product or market).

— The monetary exposure and overall risk from not conducting these tests and possibly failing are tolerable compared with the potential reward. For example, restaurants, given the high-paced competitive environment and relatively low risk, may introduce new dishes to see which ones do well and drop them if they don't catch on.

— Your company is using some type of market simulation software for new product introductions and there is sufficient data of similar products, services, and market launches, and so there is a relatively high confidence level in the accuracy of the forecast.

— Make sure you answer the question of why a slow ramp-up is not a viable option. For example, if you are a large player, why not start in the one or two of the most desirable markets where you have some competitive advantage. That way, if you are not successful there, you might want to rethink spending more money and effort as you are just increasing your exposure.

— There are downsides to testing, mainly the lost time and expense, and the very real criticism that you can tip off the competition. This last one tends to be true in highly competitive markets such as consumer packaged goods. For most others, the probability of being discovered with live tests is usually low if precautions are taken, such as introducing the product or service in markets where the competition is not present or very weak and channel partners are unlikely to divulge details and you have a plan to quickly ramp-up.

For all other cases, testing or a slow ramp-up should always be given preference, and a good case needs to be made for bypassing it, assigning a risk probability as well as monetary and opportunity exposure if the venture fails. The do's and don'ts of testing and experiments in business are well known; some of which we have already covered. Best practices in testing are neither a novel concept nor a domain transfer to business. However, just to summarize, here are a few best practices:

- Estimate the full cost and time involved in doing the test and the cost and risk of failing if no testing is conducted.
- The validity and representativeness of the test. One vital consideration is whether the product or service awareness level and distribution reach in the test is comparable to what will occur in the "real world." For example, will the results from a test done in a small rural town with a population of 10,000 be replicated when the product is launched in a major city.
- Accounting for distortions. Some percentage of the results should be discounted due to it being done under highly controlled circumstances (heightened situational awareness). Factors that could distort the test are the location (both store location and city, state, region), timing (from hour and day of the week to seasonality), and competitive response or lack of a response.

Also when testing (or if conducting an experiment or building a model), consider adding variables you don't normally look at. Sophisticated companies and agencies look at those variables on a somewhat regular basis. If you don't, consider looking at nontraditional metrics such as returns by demographic (e.g., gender, age, region), profitability by platform (web only, brick-and-mortar only, both), by acquisition mode (social media PPC, social media organic, SEO), and experiment with different ratios. For example, online retailers might not think that weather and temperature variations play much of a role. Analyze this new data to determine if (or which) temperature ranges might correlate with a measurably significant increase or decrease in sales. In which case, perhaps you should spend more money on say PPC advertising when a favorable weather pattern is present.

Ratios are extensively used in finance, often as predictors of a possible business failure. This is another area ripe with opportunity and promise for adapting and conducting a domain transfer into other areas of business. The beauty of ratios is that they are simple to calculate, unlike complex predictive models.

- **The immediacy blindspot:** You've probably heard the joke about the big city consultant who approaches the rancher with a challenge, and after complex calculations tells him how many cows he has, a fact the rancher already knew. This can be a common problem. After thousands of dollars and time, analysts may end up recommending or identifying something that is already known, of little or no consequence, is not actionable (e.g., psychographic segmentation), or is not cost-effective to implement. In part, it is not easy to always find that transformational nugget. The following are some suggestions that can help when searching for valuable insights or making recommendations:

— Usually, we stop at the immediate or proximate outcome and fail to drill-down or "flush it out" down to the root problem. When speaking with the vice president of a marketing analytics agency regarding why a certain credit card company "carpet bombs" existing customers with pitches designed for noncustomers, the explanation given was that this company had concluded that the cost and time needed to cleanse their list on a regular basis was higher than the cost of mailing out the letters. The problem with this logic is that if I'm a current customer and receive three irrelevant "new customer" letters in a row, I would automatically discard any future letters from that company without opening or reading them, including that fourth one, even though it was a relevant offer for me as a current customer. The "behavioral learning" effect being created is something they probably didn't foresee during their cost-per-letter analysis. Returning to the previous example of the airlines adding additional rows of seats, if they insist on reducing leg space, perhaps they should also disable or reduce how much a seat can be reclined—another case of not thinking through all the outcomes and possible solutions to mitigate negative impacts. Don't be the person making recommendations that haven't been thought out as thoroughly as possible.

— Another problem is when a new trend becomes the immediate and sole focus of all efforts despite the fact that valid business use cases and practices are still a work in progress and the kinks have yet to be worked out. This status currently applies to big data. Although there is little doubt it holds tremendous potential for improving operational and product efficiencies, truly transformational outcomes are yet to be revealed. Throughout history, the most revolutionary products and ideas such as the airplane, space travel, the Internet, or personal computer did not require big data to facilitate their discovery. To paraphrase a colleague, how much big data did Galileo or Newton need? Critical thinking and innovation should always be the primary focus of our efforts. Even among those areas not tasked with innovation, such as in a marketing, sales, or the analytics department, at least 10 percent of their time should be focused on identifying and suggesting way to improve the product or service offering. These departments would benefit greatly from courses in innovation. In the Epilogue, I discuss the fork in the road we are fast approaching with some potentially transformational areas such as the Internet of Things, big data, innovation, and critical thinking with the advent of artificial intelligence.

- **The less-beaten path:** In market research, surveys include importance questions that usually include the most obvious attributes, but these can obfuscate, minimize, or hide potential differentiators. For example, if selling an antacid, effective relief will always be the most important attribute. Some slight trade-off is possible with another attribute, but relief will always remain at the forefront. If there are one or two must-have attributes that have been extensively analyzed and no key differentiator found, it might make sense to leave those out of importance and ranking questions and replace them with additional attributes.[9]

The main reason is that if there is one dominant attribute—pain relief—it detracts the focus of the respondent from other attributes. When all the attention is given to the top one or two attributes, an anchoring effect is created. Attributes such as packaging, pill size, or after-taste might not get their due consideration under the shadow of the main attributes. Even with a conjoint analysis, this might be an issue. If there is a strong belief that the main attribute must be included, conduct a split test, with one group having the main attributes versus a test group without it, and then compare them to see whether the alternative attributes match in both groups.

- **Focus on key success drivers:** Because companies seldom go beyond the immediate or proximate cause, they often overlook the underlying drivers of success. For example, if you're a food or chemical company, you probably collect and analyze performance data by SKU, category, store, revenues, costs, and so on. These are necessary, but step back and see what the underlying root cause driver(s) of success is/are. The items listed previously are consequences, outcomes, or ancillary factors. In the case of food products, one key driver of success is taste, whereas in the case of chemicals it is performance. Therefore, you want to make sure that you include data that would capture any change in taste or performance. Include and track fields that would indicate whether there were any ingredient, formula, or supplier changes. Perhaps your sales went down and no promotional, competitive, or other variable seems to explain this, but it just so happens you recently modified or substituted an ingredient (or changed vendors who used different ingredients). Think about how difficult and time-consuming it would be if you were focusing only on the data available to figure out the cause of this problem (advertising, promotion, pricing, etc.). A large-scale survey might pick up on the taste issue, but how much additional time and effort would that require versus having the key variable in your data set? Moreover, this assumes you would conduct a survey. Perhaps you incorrectly attributed the decline to a decrease in advertising that, in fact, had no causal relationship. In the meantime, more market share was lost.

The overarching emphasis in any business analysis or recommendation should ensure that it is focused on key business requirements instead of on metrics that are not as important for the main business outcomes (e.g., revenue). Suppose you are Toyota and decide to hire an agency or consultant to improve your social media presence. Often, the agency will present you with something like the table shown in Figure 5.4, which highlights the better performing brands followed by comparisons of what others are doing with their social media compared to what you are doing, followed by recommendations on how to bridge the gap (better content, regularity of postings, etc.). In this example, the better performing benchmarks are BMW, Audi, and even Porsche when compared to Toyota.

Now let us see how this measures up against our key business requirement—selling more cars. To do so, we need to add data not originally provided, such as the number of units sold per year in the United States, which is inserted into Figure 5.5 next to one of the social media metrics.

Social Media

	Facebook Likes	Twitter Followers	YouTube Subscribers
Audi USA	9.14MM	831.4K	67.1K
BMW	18.40MM	441.4K	397.5K
Chevrolet	3.27MM	478.1K	296.3K
Dodge	3.00MM	312.1K	39.9K
Mercedes-Benz	15.67MM	576.7K	158.5K
Porsche	9.10MM	601.2K	203.6K
Toyota USA	2.14MM	319.1K	60.8K
Volkswagen USA	2.92MM	293.1K	86.5K

Figure 5.4 Example of a typical social media analysis

Social Media

	Facebook Likes	# of cars sold per year*
Audi USA	9.14MM	163,000
BMW	18.40MM	298,000
Chevrolet-GM	3.27MM	1,680,000
Dodge	3.00MM	1,050,000
Mercedes-Benz	15.67MM	318,000
Porsche	9.10MM	44,000
Toyota USA	2.14MM	2,158,000
Volkswagen USA	2.92MM	332,000

*Source for auto sales data: *Wall Street Journal*, June 2015

Figure 5.5 Example of a social media analysis that focuses on a key success driver

We should also bring in some consumer behavior considerations into the analysis. For example, is every brand listed a competitor of Toyota? Could it be that in some categories the numbers are skewed due to the fact that most of these social media fans (e.g., Porsche) are neither current nor prospective buyers but rather aspirational car lovers? With 44,000 cars sold per year versus Toyota's 2.1 million, is imitating Porsche's social media efforts relevant or useful? For this category, what should instead be done is to find a more relevant competitor such as Honda. Better yet, look at a comparable brand that has improved its social media year after year (i.e., more followers, fans, subscribers, etc.) and determine whether that translated into more cars being sold. If that's not the case, would such an effort be the best use of your money and effort?

As a matter of fact, many businesses might not realize that in the case of Facebook, less than 2 percent of their posts will appear in the feeds of their fans. Another reality check: One of IBM's Black Friday e-commerce reports[10] highlighted the problem with social media not contributing directly to sales, with less than 1 percent of e-commerce customers who purchased something coming from a social media site. To be fair, it is true that social media gets less credit in part because it is hard to measure what credit a sale should get when someone first hears about the product in social media and buys it several days or weeks later after conducting a Google search. However, a 2013 Gallup poll asked consumers what influence social media had on their purchases, 62 percent of those surveyed said it had no influence, and 30 percent answered "some influence." The results were only slightly better with Millennials, with 48 percent saying no influence and 43 percent stating it had some influence.[11] While social media has a role in creating awareness and interest—at the top of the sales funnel—for small businesses, a better payback might be achieved by simply improving and managing customer review sites. Social media does play a role in search engine optimization, but the benefits in this area have to be measured against the payback and *return on investment* (ROI) of other alternatives.

Problem 3: The Purchase Intent Fallacy

> *"The road to hell is paved with good intentions"*
>
> —Anonymous

One problem that bedeviled me during a certain part of my career is something I call the *purchase intent fallacy.* Companies often base pricing and/or go-to-market decisions on purchase intent survey questions; often taking them pretty much at full or close to full face value. Usually, prospects are asked questions with a Likert-type scale for responses (1–5 is common, where 1 represents not very likely to buy and 5 means very likely to buy) about the likelihood they would buy a given product or service. Often, two to three different price points are thrown in to see which gets the better response. Not surprisingly, the lower price option usually wins.

The problem with these "likelihood to buy" questions is that they are highly unreliable. Numerous studies have shown that at least in our culture, most people wish to be polite; this phenomenon is even greater among some ethnicities (e.g., Hispanics).[12] Why contradict or upset the interviewer when we don't have to buy anything since there is zero commitment? There are numerous elements at play when people are asked a "how likely is it that you would purchase product X" type of question. Respondents often have no hands-on experience with the product (e.g., Iridium), so it's a completely hypothetical scenario. In other cases, they do not wish to appear cheap or rude, preferring instead to be seen as altruistic, generous, and polite.

In addition, if these types of questions are being asked of respondents who are being paid (and often fed), another bias is being triggered, called the *reciprocity bias.* When somebody does something for us or gives us something, most people are inclined to respond in kind. This is a well-documented and exploited technique by charities that send the free return address labels or the Hare Krishna's when they used to hand out free roses at airports. How likely is it that a focus group participant will state, "There's no way I would ever buy your product, but I'll have another helping of your potato salad." To further complicate matters, those asking the questions are usually selected for being attractive, friendly, and polite, so there is also a *likeability bias* at work. This likeability factor is easier to see in network marketing. Think of the Tupperware or Avon effect when a friend or neighbor asks you to attend a house party or buy something; it's much harder to say no.

Microsoft committed this deadly sin during its prelaunch research for SPOT, a quasi-smart watch introduced in 2003. For one thing, its research relied on online Internet surveys (with subjects unable to use the prototypes) and focus groups. Moreover, the limited hands-on testing was conducted with Microsoft employees who did *not* have to purchase the watch. It should come as no surprise, then, that the responses to the purchase intent question for SPOT had a whopping 49 percent in the "very likely" or "somewhat likely" response categories. Yet when launched, SPOT was a resounding flop.[13] Where did that 49 percent of likely-to-buy purchasers go? Well, they never existed. The monetary losses were never released by Microsoft, but after five years on the market, SPOT was quietly discontinued.

Solution: "Use it and buy it." One excellent way to determine purchase intent is to have the customers try the product, and see whether they will buy it with their money. One approach to measure this is through sales wave testing, whereby you give a large group of prospects the product to try for some reasonable amount of time, have them bring it back, provide feedback, and at that time ask if they would be willing to buy the product at some predetermined price point, and determine what percentage actually purchased the product. If testing several price points, conduct several "waves" using different price points, and for each additional wave, use a new group of test subjects until you determine the optimal price point.

This technique is definitely time-consuming, but a much better way to get real purchase intent data without having to conduct a large-scale test or conduct complicated marketing simulation models. Although sales-wave tests aren't usually conducted using large samples of prospects, and therefore are not statistically significant, the realism inherent in this approach makes it worthwhile. Nothing is as good as the real thing, but this goes further in replicating real-world scenarios than a purchase intent question with 2,000 respondents. Think about this for a moment: If you had been given the iPod before it was introduced, wouldn't you have jumped at the chance to buy it?

There is one group of products, however, that might do poorly in sales-wave tests yet turn out to be a winner. These are fad products or those that rely heavily on word of mouth (network marketing); in these cases, the probability of success may not be known until out in the "real world," where word of mouth, the likeability bias, and follower instinct take over, things not easily replicated with this smaller and usually non-interconnected sample.

If you still want to ask purchase intent questions, use them for exploratory purposes only, or to identify negative sentiment. Agencies and companies that use market simulation software will calibrate purchase intent responses based on their past experiences, often reducing by a significant percentage the stated-to-actual intent to purchase responses. For others, it is best to ignore, or take with the proverbial grain of salt, any large positive sentiment. If a significant percentage of respondents, despite all the false positives inherent in this type of research, state they would not buy your product, you may have a problem. Nevertheless, they might change their minds if they used the product, so it's still hard to beat the "use it" experience. Another possible technique to minimize the likeability or nice guy bias is to present several products at once to the test subjects and not reveal which one is yours.

Problem 4: Correlation Does Not Imply Causation

> *"Trust not too much to appearances"*
>
> —Virgil

One frequent pitfall for business people is that as humans we are inclined to see patterns, often where none exist. Perhaps you observed that female customers from the southwestern region have larger-than-average order sizes. This might be true, or just a coincidence that does not repeat itself after a few more weeks or months. The reason is that in many cases, for a relationship to be valid, it must withstand the passage of time and additional observations. For example, the probability that a coin will be heads or tails is 50/50, even though you might get nine straight "heads" in a row.

In business, companies use statistical techniques (regression analysis) to try to identify relationships and patterns that can benefit their efforts. Companies try, for example, to determine which offer (15 percent off or free shipping), campaign (radio versus direct mail), market, or customer trait (males over 45 years of age with incomes over $60,000) has the biggest impact on revenue or profitability. By running these regressions, often using multiple variables, a company might come to the conclusion that an increase in radio advertising, for example, played the biggest role in increasing revenue during the past quarter. One problem with this approach is that despite the fact the correlation value might be high (e.g., anything between a .7 and 1), it might just be a coincidence. This problem has given rise to the sage advice of "correlation does not always equal causation." In this example, perhaps the radio ads were a coincidence and did not play any role in increasing revenue. There are many examples of these often purely spurious relationships.

In Figure 5.6, the first chart shows a regression where we see that the number of people who die by falling down the stairs over a six-year period closely correlates with Apple iPhone sales. In a case like this, it is relatively easy to conclude the correlation is a coincidence, with no cause-and-effect relationship (unless it is discovered that most of those who fell down the stairs and died were using an iPhone at the time). In the bottom chart, the increase in Apple iPhone sales correlates with Black Friday online revenues, which requires some additional thought before reaching a conclusion. I will come back to this correlation.

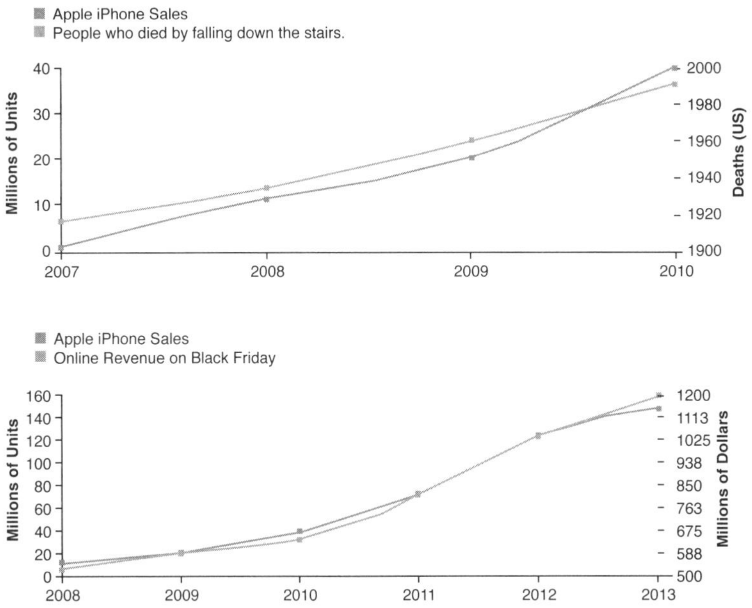

Figure 5.6 Example of highly correlated observations that have no cause-effect relationship (Source: *Spurious Relationships*, by Tyler Vigen)

One way to experience this phenomenon first hand is by using Google Correlate, a free web tool that enables you to see which keywords are highly correlated with other search keywords. The idea is that if you want to advertise something like pizza through a PPC ad, you may want to consider bidding on other keywords showing a strong correlation with the keyword "pizza," such as the keyword phrase "tonight's football game." If we run a query using the keyword "order pizza," we get many highly correlated terms that probably have some relationship with the keyword "pizza," including brand names such as Dominos or Papa John's. Others take a bit more consideration to figure out a connection to pizza, such as Thai food. In this case, the correlation probably has to do with people trying to decide what type of food they want: pizza or Thai. Other correlated keywords, however, appear to make no sense at all.

Table 5.1 shows many of these correlations, some making sense, others like "boy names," which despite having a .97 correlation, seem to have no cause-and-effect relationship. In this as in many cases, if you simply extend the time frame, the correlation disappears. When this occurs, usually either the correlation was just happenstance, with no cause-effect relationship, or it was of such short duration that it is probably not very useful in any business initiative.

Table 5.1 Example of Keywords Correlated with the Keyword "Pizza"

.9894	Village pizza
.9890	Pizza hut
.9842	Dominos
.9830	Thai foods
.9802	NY pizza
.9780	Boy names

Source: Data from Google Correlate

Another possibility is that they don't have a cause-effect relationship with each other but do have a shared cause, such as seasonality. This explanation is plausible if it withstands the test of time. For example, an increase in winter clothing sales and an increase in gas explosions are closely correlated year after year. However common sense tell us there is no probable cause-effect relationship between them. There's no way an increase in winter clothing sales could cause gas explosions. Conversely, an increase in gas explosions should not result in an increase in winter clothing sales. In this case, there is no relationship between each other, but each individual effect *is* highly correlated to cold temperatures, which tend to occur during the winter months year after year. When it is cold more people use their gas furnaces, and inevitably some will explode. Both effects thus share a cause (cold temperatures) but do not play any role in causing each other.

In Figure 5.6, we saw that the increase in iPhone sales showed a correlation with an increase in Black Friday online revenues. These events, however, are more likely to share a common cause than a cause-effect type of relationship; perhaps an improvement in the economy, as well as the growing interest in new gadgets and electronics by those who shop online during the holidays. The problem when you have a shared cause situation is that often there is no relevant business insight you can leverage to your benefit.

So while the lack of a cause-effect relationship is evident in the pizza and winter clothing examples, in other cases determining whether the correlation is merely a coincidence is not as straightforward. What if a 10 percent increase in advertising expenditures correlated with an increase in revenues? There could be a cause-effect relationship, be a coincidence, or they could share a common cause.

Solution: The goal is to see whether there is a cause-effect relationship. If there is, see if you can leverage the knowledge into a business initiative. How you might go about trying to determine whether there is a cause-effect relationship is illustrated in Figure 5.7. As mentioned previously, one option is to let the passage of time prove or disprove if the causation exists. As time goes by, the correlation will disappear if there was no relationship. Complications include not having historic data, or relying on a small sample size, or that it may require months or years to prove or disprove the relationship when there is not enough data. One such case is the Super Bowl Indicator, which is based on the observation that if a football team from the old AFL (AFC division) wins the Super Bowl, the next year will be a bear market, whereas a win for a former NFC division team means a bull stock market year. Does it work? Well, it depends on what time frame you choose, but it has been correct 33 out of 41 times. Clearly, the Super Bowl Indicator is just a coincidence, with no cause-effect or shared causation. In 2008, when the Giants—an NFC team—won, what should have been a bull year turned out to be the worst year for the stock market since the Great Depression. What allows this indicator to have an above-average success rate is that it relies on a once-a-year game between only two teams.

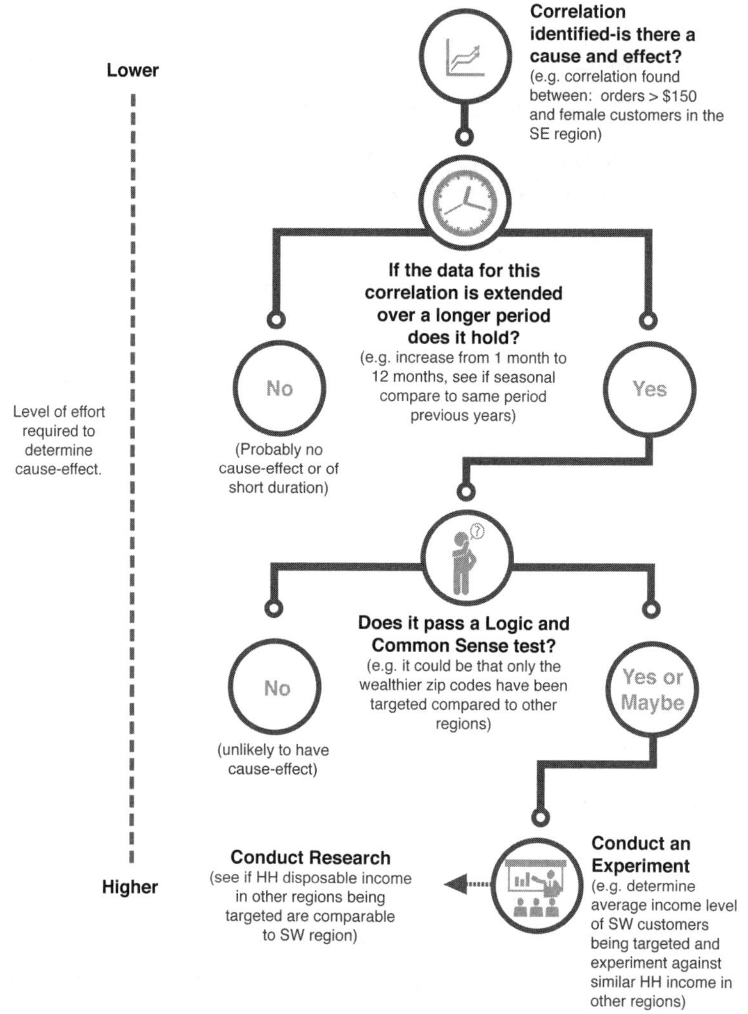

Figure 5.7 Identifying a causal relationship

One can also attempt to find a causal explanation using the RCA technique explored in the previous chapter. For some cases, a dose of logic and common sense can go a long way, as was the case with the winter clothing and gas explosion example. With the advent of big data, and the availability of thousands of variables and large bodies of data, the potential for false positives (correlations with no causation) will continue to grow exponentially. As a result, companies like Google are focusing their efforts on conducting ongoing experiments with large data sets over certain time periods. For example, will running a pizza ad triggered by the keyword "boys name" generate more clicks or conversions than other experimental keywords such as "football game tonight" versus the tried-and-true control keyword "order pizza."

Problem 5: Cherry-Picked Data

> *"The more people rationalize cheating, the more it becomes a culture of dishonesty. And that can become a vicious, downward cycle. Because suddenly, if everyone else is cheating, you feel a need to cheat, too."*
>
> —Stephen Covey

Everyone knows cherry-picking takes place often, but one would be hard pressed to quantify how widespread the problem is. For one thing, it often goes undetected, and when it is identified, it's usually kept within the confines of the parties involved. The only time cherry-picking sees the light of public scrutiny is when a government or a large corporation gets caught selectively reporting their intelligence or financial data or if the safety or health of consumers is in danger.

Cherry-picking is something most everyone in business or research has probably done at one time or another in his or her career. When promotions, reputations, bonuses, or even your job are at stake, the temptation to cherry-pick is strong and easy to rationalize with all sorts of justifications (e.g., the spike or dip was a fluke). This inclination is not something a mandatory HR ethics webinar can solve.

This scenario, unfortunately, occurs frequently in pharmaceutical companies, which, to get FDA approval or physician buy-in, resort to cherry-picking their studies and findings. A *Scientific American* article titled "Trial Sans Error: How Pharma-Funded Research Cherry-Picks Positive Results" concluded the following: "Clinical trial data on new drugs is systematically withheld from doctors and patients, bringing into question many of the premises of the pharmaceutical industry—and the medicine we use."[14]

One infamous case occurred when Pfizer-Pharmacia, realizing that their drug Celebrex was no more effective than other pain relief drugs on the market, made a case for FDA approval on the basis that Celebrex was "easier on the stomach" than drugs currently on the market. To accomplish this, Pfizer cherry-picked its findings using only the first 6 months out of a 12-month study. The full 12 months showed it was no easier on the stomach than the other drugs. The *New York Times* reported how "Documents show that in February 2000, Pharmacia employees came up with a game plan on how they might present the findings once they were available. 'Worse case: we have to attack the trial design if we do not see the results we want,' a memo read. It went on: 'If other endpoints do not deliver, we will also need to strategize on how we provide the data.' [...] Another document, a slide, proposed explaining poor results through 'statistical glitches.'"[15] The Ioannidis Prophesy comes to mind regarding what happens to research when there is a desired outcome by management.

Solution: Unless there is a predetermined and agreed upon set of metrics and protocols about what data must be included or excluded, cherry-picking might have to be given the benefit of the doubt. There should be a set of reporting metrics agreed upon by upper management and collected by a department or individual with no conflict of interest (e.g., bonuses or promotions). Any change to these metrics should be well documented and approved by the appropriate parties.

Missing data: Usually it boils down to asking many of the questions listed in problem 2 regarding missing data, along with the following:

- The first question should be, "Is this *all* the data and research conducted?" If something was left out, find out why. Data left out should be a red or at least a yellow flag. As was seen in the Celebrex example, minor flaws are often built in and can later be highlighted if the outcome is adverse, or ignored if the desired results were obtained.
- Make sure that assumptions are listed and have been verified.
- Make sure that the right success drivers to your particular business strategy and objectives are present. If profitability is your goal, an increase in market share might hide bad news.

Graphs: A lot of shenanigans can take place with graphs, so here are some tips:

- Carefully review the graph's interval; pay close attention if the intervals do not start at zero. The chart in Figure 5.8a can make the increase in unit sales more significant than what it is when it is compared against the chart in Figure 5.8b.

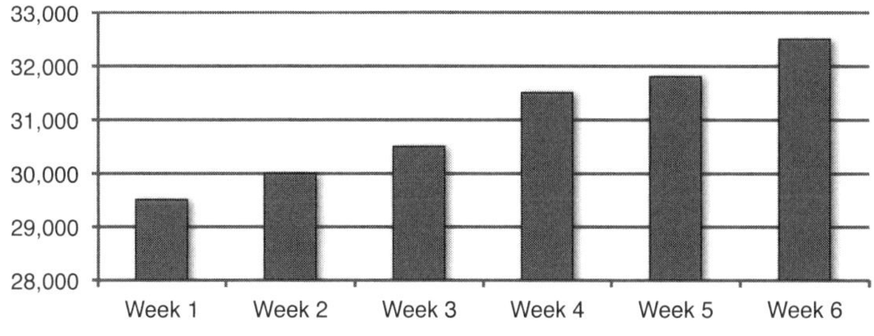

Figure 5.8a Product A with interval starting at 28,000

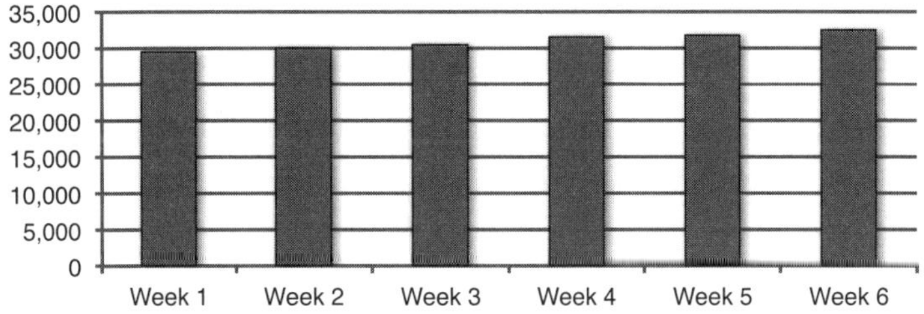

Figure 5.8b Product A with interval starting at zero

Another common problem is the use of convoluted graphs. Data-heavy or hard-to-decipher graphs may hide bad news or obfuscate important trends. The example in Figure 5.9 shows how the radar chart is hard to decipher, while the same data can be represented in an easy-to-analyze table. If a percentage difference had also been shown in the table, it would have been even easier to detect the trends. The whole objective of charts and graphs is to make the interpretation of data easier to facilitate the decision-making process. Anyone presented with a data-heavy radar chart like the one pictured should ask for the table version. Unfortunately, most managers feel self-conscious when they see a data-heavy or confusing chart and can't quickly determine the insight, so they remain silent.

- **Percentages:** Be suspicious of percentages if they do not also display the number of units upon which the percentage is based, or fail to compare the current data against other time periods or forecasts. Percentages can be very helpful, but can easily be misleading as well. For example, Figure 5.10 shows a large percentage increase in revenue for products A and B, while product C appears to be underperforming. Figure 5.11 uses the exact same data as Figure 5.10, but this time it is expressed in units instead of as a percentage. A very different story now emerges, with products A and B showing a very mediocre improvement in terms of the number of units sold during the second year. Product C, however, is carrying the company despite its modest percentage growth rate. Percentages are best used for pie charts when used to compare one variable as a part of the whole (e.g., males 47 percent, females 53 percent) or presented side by side with the underlying data.

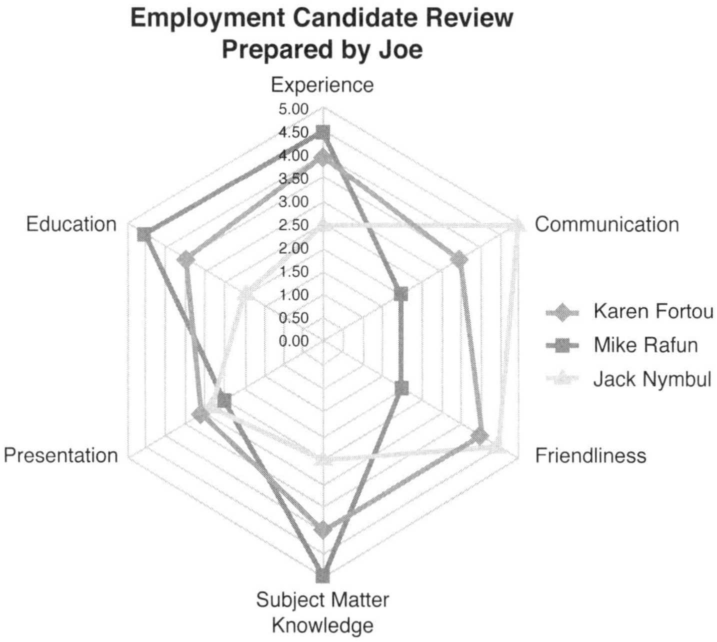

Employment Candidate Review

	Candidates		
Rating Areas	Karen Fortou	Mike Rafun	Jack Nymbul
Experience	4.00	4.50	2.50
Communication	3.50	2.00	5.00
Friendliness	4.00	2.00	4.50
Subject Matter Knowledge	4.00	5.00	2.50
Presentation	3.00	1.50	2.75
Education	3.50	4.50	2.00
Average Rating	3.67	3.25	3.21

Figure 5.9 Employment candidate review (Source: *Show Me the Numbers* by Stephen Few)

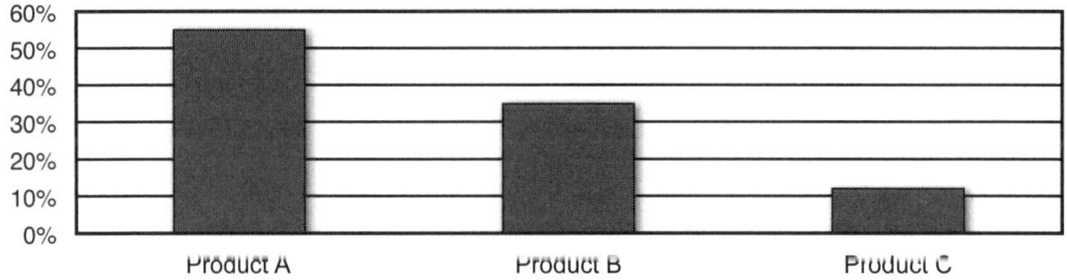

Figure 5.10 Percent revenue growth for year 2 (compared with year 1)

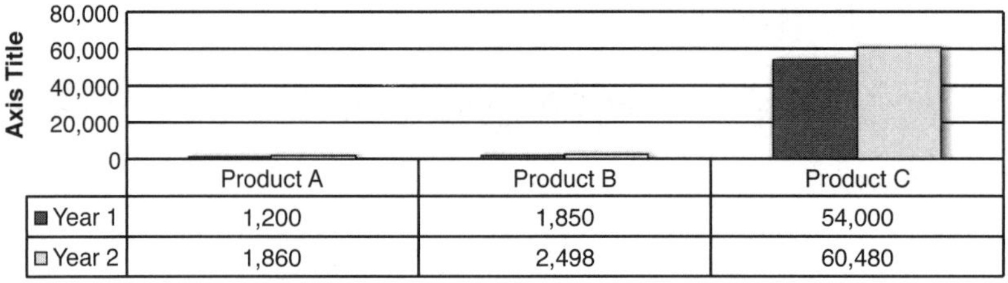

Figure 5.11 Revenue growth (current versus last year) in units

As the availability of data continues to grow exponentially, it will become increasingly important for managers to identify potential issues and problems with how the data is represented. The problems can be of two types: poor data visualization techniques or skewed graphs that are attempting to either hide bad news or exaggerate relatively inconsequential success. One excellent resource is Stephen Few's book, *Show Me the Numbers.*[16]

Problem 6: The Shiny Object Compulsion and Losing Sight of the "Basics"

> *"Efficiency is doing things right; effectiveness is doing the right things"*
>
> —Peter Drucker

Our minds are conditioned by technology success stories and the subsequent pursuit of the latest hyped idea or product to reject simple but effective solutions. We assume that we need to focus on intricate, complicated, and often expensive approaches to improve our business, products, and campaigns. In addition to domain transfers proven in other disciplines, very often a simple analysis of how you are performing on the basic success drivers (e.g., delivery time) can be more effective than untested new alternatives. Here are a few examples in healthcare and business:

- Robotic surgery—with the da Vinci System being the market leader—was introduced into medicine in the mid-1980s. These robotic devices cost millions of dollars and require extensive training and servicing. Approximately one-fourth of hospitals offer some form of robotic surgery, driven to a great extent by the need to differentiate them from the competition by offering cutting-edge technology. However, the actual efficacy and *return on investment* (ROI) of current robotic surgery technology is mixed. A 2010 study found that 57 percent of surgeons surveyed anonymously said, "They had experienced irrecoverable operative malfunctions while using the da Vinci System."[17] In March 2013, the American Congress of Obstetricians and Gynecologists released the following strongly worded statement: "There is no good data proving that robotic hysterectomy is even as good as—let alone better than—existing, and far less costly, minimally invasive alternatives."[18] Compare these results to the quick, low-cost, and effective reduction in infections and deaths from the implementation of a simple checklist at the Johns Hopkins Hospital.
- A healthcare experiment case study from 2002 (not 1902) in Karachi, Pakistan, used a test group of children and parents who were taught, reminded, and monitored about proper hand-washing techniques versus a control group that received no such training or monitoring. It's hard to get more mundane

> than proper hand washing in the 21st century. Compared to the control group, this simple act reduced the incidence of pneumonia in children by approximately 47 percent, impetigo skin infections by 45 percent, and diarrhea by 52 percent![19] There aren't many pharmaceutical products that can claim that type of effective and inexpensive result with no side effects.

In business, we experience our fair share of the "shiny new object" mentality. Many companies, both large and small, jump on the social media widget of the week—e.g., Instagram or WhatsApp—without any clear strategy or understanding of its strengths and weaknesses. The labor and opportunity costs of the time spent creating numerous social media accounts, pages, posts, tweets, and images that few people see, share, or more importantly that fail to motivate prospects to make a purchase, would make for an interesting study. In some high-involvement and engagement categories such as entertainment or food verticals, it may be time well spent. However, one often sees small commodity type businesses (e.g., a dry cleaner) asking customers to "Like" them on Facebook, with the expectation that people will be engaged by their posts, sharing them with friends who will in turn do business with the dry cleaner. Many businesses are slowly disabusing themselves of the shiny object compulsion that has no demonstrable payback.

Solution: The basics first!

When Vince Lombardi took over the until-then losing Green Bay Packers football team, he was asked what he was going to change. The players, the strategy, the plays, or the training? Lombardi replied that he wouldn't change any of these but would instead concentrate on being "brilliant on the basics." Companies would do well to follow this advice and conduct a finance, operations, sales, marketing, and customer service audit of their company. What happens if someone goes to the website form and requests information? What happens when someone calls ten minutes before closing time; will anyone answer in a timely manner? I recently attempted to get additional information from a Fortune 500 company on their "lead generation" software. I called several times, during regular business hours, and each call went straight to the voicemail of an individual instead of to a shared voicemail so that others could retrieve messages. I also sent numerous emails. I would have filled out an online form as well, but received a "404 Page not found" error. Fast forward two months later—I never received any response (and no, they didn't prequalify me). This can happen with small, medium-size, and large-sized companies. The true test is when a nonstandard inquiry or question is made (e.g., "can I change this or that functionality to do X or Y?"). A quick and correct response for an unorthodox inquiry is where many large companies flounder, making it a good litmus test for any company.

Another example and solution: Companies often spend a significant amount of time and effort improving their social media and PPC advertising campaigns only to eventually find that their conversion rates and overall online sales have not improved. The focus should be on *which* of these options offers the best and fastest payback. The sequence illustrated in Figure 5.12 offers the best payback in descending order, with usability at the pinnacle. Naturally, at some stage you will reach a point of diminishing returns. After many iterations and usability redesigns, you will eventually reach a point where additional time and effort spent in this area will produce only a marginal lift if any in sales. The order of priorities shown in Figure 5.12 are self- explanatory and obvious. For example, what is the point in spending money or time in achieving a great PPC advertising campaign, achieving a high organic page ranking, or social media campaign if your website is slow, or your products are difficult to find, or the navigation is confusing, or the shopping cart has a technical bug and therefore a high cart abandonment rate?

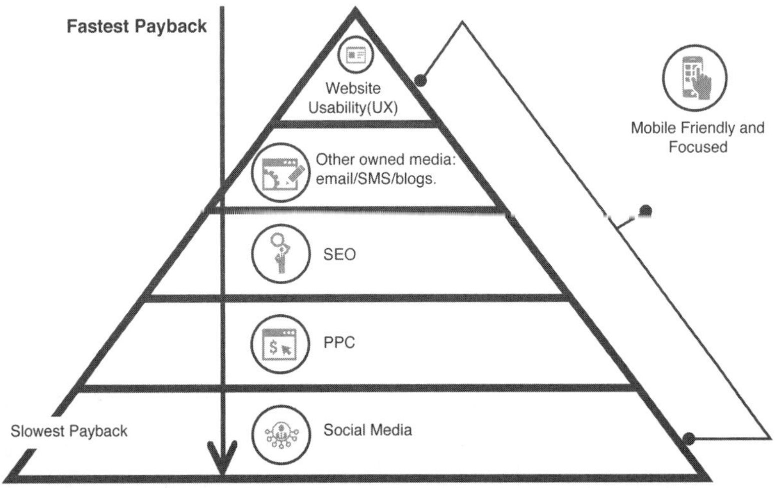

Figure 5.12 Payback funnel in digital

While Drucker designated innovation and marketing as the two most essential functions in a business, many would say the Sales department is just as important. Sales is an area rife with opportunity for many of the failure techniques discussed in the book and where the basics are often ignored, especially in small and medium-sized companies. Technology and pharmaceutical companies tend to have sophisticated sales training, CRM systems, and compensation programs. For the rest, the basics in selling are often overlooked, including product knowledge, competency, closing techniques, and empathy (empathy, however, in the context of the willingness to work to resolve a customer's need, regardless of whether it results in the short term in a sale).

In addition to problems with training or lack of CRM software, a more frequent and basic flaw are problems in the conversion process. You saw in Chapter 2, "Don't Start Off on the Wrong Foot," how one of the most useful techniques is to drill down or break down a process into smaller components (in the case of sales, by creating a conversion funnel so that performance can be benchmarked and corrective action taken). The funnel shown in Figure 5.13 does this by comparing the best performing salesperson against the average performance. (It would be better to compare it against each salesperson.) By breaking down the process into smaller components, it is now very easy to identify that the problem in this example exists in the final stage, which is how many quotes result in sales.

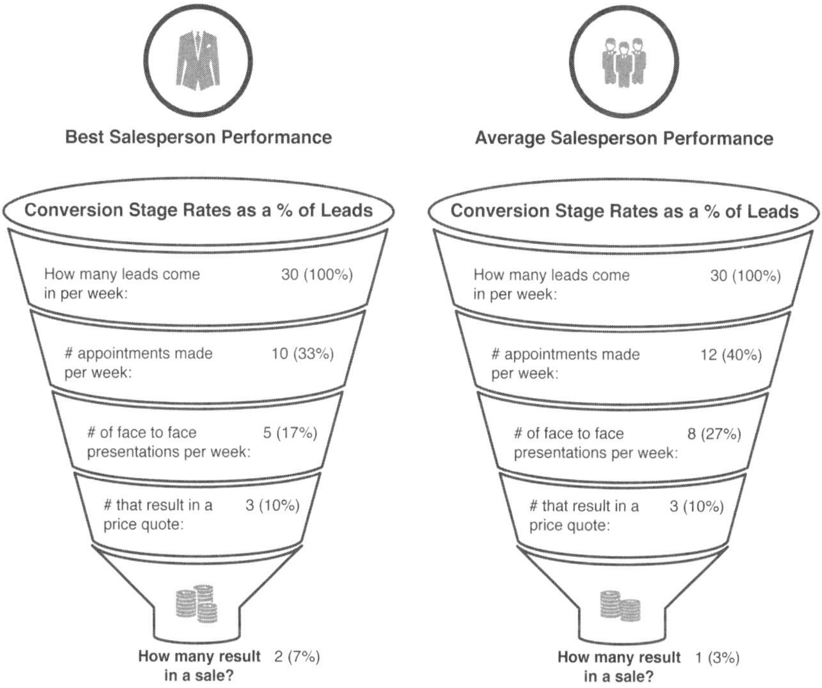

Figure 5.13 Breaking down the sales funnel into components for troubleshooting

This breakdown and the identification of where the problem resides allows you to now perform a simple RCA to determine the underlying cause. Is it poor quality or incomplete or incorrectly calculated quotes? Or is it a lack of follow-up after the quote is sent? By comparing the quotes of the best salesperson to that of other salespeople and their follow-up communications (e.g., using CRM-contact management software), the underlying cause might be uncovered and corrected. If the answer is not there, go back one stage. Perhaps the sales representative did a decent job presenting but did not handle objections well, and so while they accepted a quote, they might have already made up their mind against buying (the root cause being poor training in closing techniques and handling objections).

Hopefully, companies will consider implementing effective and simple techniques from other domains and rediscover the basics so as to reduce the prevailing failure and underperformance rates. True, at some stage all the simple ideas and techniques will have been transferred and adopted, but that point is still very far away. The FMEA is in particular (along with an RCA when failure or underperformance occurs) one of the best ways to make sure that you are doing the "basics" well, especially when you successfully identify what controls and detection mechanisms are in place or are missing (e.g., training).

The Tesco "Fresh & Easy" Case Study: A $3 Billion Failure

Tesco is a British supermarket conglomerate that is ranked as the second largest in the world, with $101.2 billion in sales and operations in 12 countries. In 2007, Tesco decided to expand into the U.S. market through the brand Fresh & Easy. The company is well known for its use of analytics and loyalty programs and for conducting impeccable market research, and the U.S. launch was no exception. Senior executives went to live and interact with Californian families to observe their shopping and eating behaviors and preferences. They even built secret test stores. Five years later, and with some 200 stores, Tesco called it quits with accumulated losses in five years totaling some $3.1 billion.

The causes for failure, without the benefit of an RCA, have been summarized as three proximate causes in several magazine articles, to which I suggest some underlying causes:[20]

- **Timing:** Tesco entered the U.S. market at around the same time as the biggest recession since the Great Depression started and were located in some of the states hardest hit by the mortgage implosion, such as Arizona and Nevada.

  Root cause: This might be somewhat of an known-unknown, given that this company was not an investment banker speculating in hedge funds but rather a British company entering the U.S. market. However, 200 stores was no slow ramp-up, which if done could have mitigated its downside risk. Tesco should have picked the best geographic market and made it happen there or called it quits. If they had done this, their losses would have been significantly less.

- **Poor choice of locations:** Tesco discovered that finding prime locations was very difficult in the hypercompetitive American market. It locked in locations before the crash, when real estate was tight and expensive.

  Root cause: This failure is inexcusable. What research and process did the company use when choosing locations? Did they not identify this as a potential market entry problem? A FMEA for store location selection in a particular market would have probably identified this as a major risk and fact that there were no controls in place to address or detect this potential cause of failure.

- **Surprisingly, Tesco ignored a lot of the research findings:** For example, the research it conducted showed that American families like to buy in bulk. However, it opted to offer mainly small package sizes, as they do in England.

  Root cause: This is one of Ioannidis's warnings: Beware when management wants the research to produce some specific outcome that fits their preconceived notions; in those cases, conflicting information will be explained away or ignored.

The "Known-Unknowns": Forecasting

> *"We really can't forecast all that well, and yet we pretend that we can, but we really can't."*
>
> —Alan Greenspan, former Chairman of the Federal Reserve.

Forecasting is the roadmap for any business, campaign, or new product launch. Without it, there is no way to measure progress or what constitutes underperformance when the goals are not being achieved. If there is no forecast, there can be no useful EWS. Unfortunately, it is also one of the most challenging areas from economics to politics, where the accuracy rate is often no better than chance. Global competition, coupled with rapidly changing consumer tastes and technologies, makes business forecasting a daunting task. One of the main obstacles to better forecasting is the lack of a continuous improvement process combined with flawed thinking. As shown in Chapter 3, when a negative outcome occurs, the focus is usually on the proximate cause (the person who made the forecast, or some "unexpected" event). More problematic is when companies fail to improve their forecasting accuracy, believing there are too many factors and unknowns at play. "It's as good as it's going to get" is a commonly heard refrain.

The belief that more resources and talented people will solve the problem is disingenuous. Leaving aside cases of fraud, of which there have been many, predictions by sophisticated entities such as hedge funds (with armies of statisticians, economists, and yes, even rocket scientists), the Federal Reserve, and banks were all far off the mark when it came to predicting the crash of 2007–2008. In fact, they learned nothing from the implosion of hedge fund Long Term Management Capital ten years earlier, which had all the complex models and risk elements seen again in 2007–2008. Long Term Management Capital didn't lack talent, either. Two of its founders were Nobel laureates, Myron Scholes and Robert Merton, whose mathematical model powered Long Term Management, which did well during the first few years, only to implode after the "unknown-unknowns" appeared.[21] Statistics works great in simple binary situations (tossing a coin) as well as in complex scenarios as long as there is sufficient historical data. The problem here was that these experts attempted to determine the risk for situations for which they did not have enough historical data, thus woefully underestimating their possible occurrence. For example, if a product failure has never occurred in a company's 30-year history, the probability rate of failure it will be assigned for this year's product launch would probably be close to zero. This is what happened to Standard and Poor's, which forecasted the default rate risk for five-year AAA-rated *collaterized debt obligations* (CDOs) at 0.12 percent, when in reality it ended up being 28 percent.[22] In another situation, leading economists who participated in the Survey of Professional Forecasters sponsored by the Philadelphia Federal Reserve thought the chance of a severe recession in 2008, expressed in terms of a decrease in the GDP, was only 1 in 500.[23]

In the late 1980s, Philip Tetlock, a psychologist and management professor from the University of Pennsylvania at Wharton, launched a project involving 284 economists, political scientists, intelligence analysts, and journalists, collecting approximately 28,000 predictions. The study found that the average expert did only slightly better than random guessing, and also highlighted the role that the *overconfidence bias* played among "experts." Tetlock observed common traits among the less versus more successful forecasters, characterizing the less successful as "hedgehogs" or big idea types who would hold on dogmatically to a frame of reference (e.g., Ron Johnson, ex-CEO of JCPenney). Hedgehogs tend to be less willing than others to change their perspectives, are overconfident, and tend to be specialists instead of generalists. Moreover, when their predictions are wrong, they attribute the failure to other factors, mainly proximate causes, unwilling to readjust their approaches or forecasts. The better forecaster type is the so-called fox, who is multidisciplinary, self-critical, cautious, and respectful of complexity and the unknowns. Their forecasts seldom have a high confidence level, and they are willing to re-examine their thinking, biases, and data—all of which are key to any continuous improvement effort.[24]

A government agency called the *Intelligence Advanced Research Projects Activity* (IARPA) has continued Tetlock's study. The project is mainly focused on political forecasting and funds numerous academic research projects. It will be interesting to see what, if any, lessons can be drawn for business forecasting. In these studies, unfortunately when a bad forecast is made no RCA is being conducted. Another issue is that the studies are ad hoc and disjointed from each other, with some discontinued after only two years. Multiyear studies are critical in forecasting given the false positives that can otherwise occur. A final challenge is that of the self-selection sample bias. In these forecasting studies, participants are volunteers who have time on their hands, something not usually found among top business professionals. If a study were being conducted for new product forecasting but without companies with a depth of forecasting expertise—as one might find at Apple, ConAgra Foods, Hewlett-Packard, Proctor & Gamble, or DuPont—any results observed would not contain an important segment of forecasters.

The *confirmation bias* discussed at the beginning of this chapter is closely related to the overconfidence effect. The useful research in this area occurs when test subjects have a good grasp of the subject matter, as occurred in Tetlock's study, which nevertheless showed a large error rate even among experts. For example, a study by the University of Nebraska found that 68 percent of faculty rated themselves in the top 25 percent in teaching ability.[25] Moreover, there's no need to rely on a study to see the cemetery of overconfident forecasters. Just look at all the failed businesses where many otherwise talented people (e.g., Tesco, Pets.com, Webvan) overestimated the likelihood of success and their own abilities.

One additional factor affecting forecasting accuracy is the type and situation under which a forecasting model is used. Table 5.2 shows different forecasting scenarios or situations.

Table 5.2 Forecasting Conditions

	Stable Environment	Volatile Environment
New Product	**Quadrant 1** If close variations exist in the marketplace (e.g., a new car model) a) < one year b) > one year	**Quadrant II** And/or no close variations exist in the market (e.g., when the PC was first launched) a) < one year b) > one year
Existing Product	**Quadrant III** e.g., the fertilizer market a) < two years b) > two years	**Quadrant IV** e.g., the next model of smartphone a) < one year b) > one year

There are a multitude of different forecasting models, each with different options or combinations of others. The reason to cover the basics of each model is so that the recommended model makes more sense:

- **Subjective or judgmental:** This is the most simple and primitive type but is often used even in sophisticated models to fill in gaps. The model is based on expert opinion, experience, and intuition. While an element of subjective forecasting is acceptable, it is dangerous as a standalone. When used, one popular technique to avoid group think is called the Delphi method, by which the experts within the company do their forecasts separately and then compare and aggregate them. The subjective forecast usually consists of a combination of market research, historical data, and judgment in varying degrees.

- **Time series/extrapolation:** In these models, past results are projected into the future and adjusted for different variables, especially time. Many different techniques are used in this category, from simplistic percentage increases, to moving averages and regressions. The details of how these forecasting models work are beyond the scope of this book. For situations like those in Quadrant III of Table 5.2 and when the forecast is for a 12-month period, extrapolation models work just fine. However, the weakness of these models should be apparent because the future might not be predicated on past events given that new factors appear (a new competitive product) and other variables take on a larger or lesser role (government regulations).
- **Causal models:** There is a wide range in this category, from sophisticated econometric models to the simpler cause-effect model introduced in the EWS. These models are constantly being revised and updated with new data. Large companies tend to use econometric causal forecasts, but these are also complex and expensive, putting them out of the reach of smaller players.

  One mini-causal type forecast seldom performed is the *return on promotion* (ROP). This simple forecast can be used for basically any promotional activity that has a cost associated with it. It is a decision tool to help you determine *a priori* if you should spend money on a public relations event, hire a sales representative, or conduct advertising, direct mail, email, PPC, or any other type of promotion. The ROP consists of an estimate of all the costs that are specific to the initiative being planned. A detailed example is provided in the Appendix in the "The Return on Promotion" section.
- **Artificial intelligence models:** These include things like neural networks driven by machine learning, which hold the most promise. This is still an emerging field, so it also needs to stand the test of time, and especially under turbulent conditions, to see whether their predictive power holds.

Improving Forecasts

Large corporations purchase or develop their own highly sophisticated forecasting software that contains various elements and combinations but which usually includes some type of causal forecast with time-series, statistical regressions, and maybe machine learning components. However, the emphasis of this book is on *simple* techniques and tools that the majority of businesses of any size can incorporate. If you are a start-up or small business without access to sophisticated forecasting software, the recommendation is to create and start using a causal forecast and, if possible, learn how to do time series analysis on past data to complement it. The basics of creating a casual forecast were covered in Chapter 4. The following are ways in which you can improve and troubleshoot your forecast:

- **Accountability:** Implement an RCA when a forecast is off by a significant percentage. Over the course of more than 25 years, I never witnessed anyone, including myself, go back and do that type of analysis. The reason for this is because it is much like a bad relationship, with all the memories and baggage. Our minds are hardwired to move on. However, if managers know that they will be held accountable for measurable improvements, they would look more closely for oversights or errors before signing off on a forecast. One additional issue is that the forecaster often has a monetary or other incentive to be optimistic. To dampen this overconfidence, the accuracy of a forecast should become a component of the forecaster's performance evaluation and bonus. A poor forecast can translate into thousands or even millions of dollars in unsellable merchandise or lost opportunities.
- **Probabilistic judgment:** In addition to assumptions, the forecast should include a detailed probabilistic judgment. For example, a product-sales forecast for year one that is $3 million might be assigned a probability of .90 by the manager and a

confidence level of 95 percent with a +/–2 margin of error. One problem is that savvy managers may or will probably start hedging their bets and lower their probability and confidence level intervals while providing the same target forecast to obtain some wiggle room should the forecast be off target. To avoid this, a minimum base or floor should be established. What that minimum should be depends on which quadrant of Table 5.2 your product is in. For situations like those in Quadrant II, the confidence level could be in the 70 percent range with a margin of error of +/–3. However, in Quadrant III in Table 5.2, one would expect a probability and confidence level of 95 percent and margin of error of <2.

One common error managers make when estimating the probability that a new product will be successful is that they often look at three or four of the launch stages, assign each a probability of success such as .8, .9, and .9, and then conclude that the overall probability of success is about a .9. The problem is that these are very often independent events occurring sequentially, with the previous stage determining whether the next one will occur. The correct calculation is .8 * .9 * .9, for a probability of .65, which is nowhere close to the earlier .9 prediction (and that is assuming these hasty mental probabilities are even correct). This oversight can create unwarranted confidence in the success of the venture. The sad thing is that this error is seldom understood. After a failed forecast, many managers will simply conclude that the probabilities were too optimistic without realizing that the erroneous calculation was another key problem in their assessment.

- **Continuous improvement:** We know the *overconfidence effect* exists in forecasts, but those who leverage something called *Bayes' theorem* can improve forecast accuracy by embracing this subjective element. Used by many analytics and research professionals, it is seldom used by marketing or product management professionals. In a Bayesian forecast model, weights initially assigned to different casual factors (prior probabilities) are adjusted after actuals come in, so there is an ongoing adjustment mechanism. Typically, what should be done is to use 24 months of historical data and then enter and assign weights to causal factors based on the first 18 months to predict the next 6 months. Because you already know the outcome of those last 6 months, note your variance and use it to recalibrate your weights and probabilities. After a few iterations, proceed with the future forecast. Causal forecasting and Bayesian methods form a strong combination. Studies have shown that Bayesian forecasts, when compared to extrapolation forecasts (regressions), have much lower rates of error.[26]

Benchmarking your forecasting accuracy rate against that of other companies ranges from difficult to impossible. Nevertheless, it can be done within a business with multiple product lines. Forecasters who consistently achieve high success rates should be used for best practices. However, the benchmark must withstand the test of time. A forecaster might be lucky for two years in a row and then have four straight years of bad predictions. While none have been proven perfect, one statistical technique used to gauge the accuracy of multiple forecasts for an event is the *Brier score.* This formula uses measurements that capture the uncertainty of the event, the reliability of the different forecasts, and the resolution (how much the conditional probabilities differ from the average). The forecast that obtains the score closest to zero is the most accurate of the forecasts.

- **Aggregate forecasts:** One additional consideration is to use the Delphi method common in judgmental forecasts, where you have several stakeholders such as sales, production, marketing, product management, and others each arrive at their own forecasts and then aggregate the results. One issue is that this would require, with our proposed model, that each person create his or her own cause-effect forecast model, which might be cumbersome. However, the aggregate forecast is often better than any individual forecast, given the overconfidence and incentive biases. Research has shown that aggregate forecasts can reduce forecasting error by as much as 20 percent. However, this does not always mean that the aggregate is better than the best individual forecast.[27]

- **The EWS, RCA, and FMEA:** Forecasting is no different from any other initiative. When a forecast fails, an RCA should be conducted. If you put in place the EWS detailed in Chapter 4, you will have a head start on diagnosing and improving your forecast. Moreover, an RCA being conducted on a forecast should always start with the assumptions and what actually occurred later. For those assumptions that were incorrect, determine the impact they may have had on the overall forecast. This might explain to a large extent the variance in your forecast. Another important area to help focus and guide your RCA is to obtain a detailed variance report of forecasted-to-actuals, especially for the key drivers. Sort these in descending order and then prioritize them based on the magnitude of difference in both percentage and units and overall impact on the forecast. For example, if you predicted a 0.5 percent response rate for display PPC and actuals were 0.3 percent, that might not appear significant. But if that translated into 3,000 fewer orders, that would be another story. The opposite could also be true, where a 25 percent variance in forecasted email orders might seem alarming until we see that the list is very new and has fewer than 500 names. This discrepancy is easily visualized in the EWS.

  The FMEA should be a part of any of the key initiatives that drive any significant percentage of your revenues. If when building a forecast you have a driver that accounts for say

25 percent of expected revenues, make sure that you have a FMEA in place for that initiative. The RCA would come into play after the actual results come in and a negative variance results.

The "Unknown–Unknowns"

"Apparently there is nothing that cannot happen today."
—Mark Twain.

Unfortunately, there is no easy solution for correctly estimating the probability of outcomes and risks such as those in Quadrant II of Table 5.2 when there is insufficient historical data. Fortunately, there are actually very few true unknown-unknowns, but it does, however, serve as a great excuse. Who can be blamed for not having predicted an unknown-unknown? The fact is that in 95 percent or more of cases in business, it's either a known-known or known-unknown that gets you into trouble. In business, there are three potential contributors to failure under the unknown-unknown scenario, as follows:

- **External events outside our domain and capabilities to monitor:** Small and medium-sized companies do not have the resources and breadth of departments or the expertise to closely monitor many of the signals and events that can negatively impact a company or product. Large companies have Market Research departments that monitor trends and the competition using the latest software and third-party vendors. Smaller-sized companies without access to these resources must create and monitor an EWS and be prepared to dial down on purchases or other commitments if the slowdown cannot be pinned down to any specific action they have taken or not taken.

- **Catastrophic events such as wars, terrorist acts, or sudden death of the principal in the business:** This is a tougher problem to be prepared for, be it a small or large company. The best option is to make sure that you have a preplanned exit strategy as detailed in the next chapter, which includes a Plan B option whereby you can retrench, contract, or focus on a different market while you weather the storm. However, if a certain negative threshold is met or the remedial actions attempted have not worked, a permanent exit strategy can be pursued.
- **Disruptive technologies:** One true unknown-unknown would be the appearance of a disruptive technology as happened in the past with the automobile, airplane, email, personal computer, smartphone, and digital media. The signals that precede an emerging disruptive technology are weak and therefore easily overlooked. Clayton Christensen, in his book *The Innovator's Dilemma,* listed some of these signals as new products or services with lower gross margins, smaller target markets, and without the features current customers seemed to desire. He suggests that large companies, the most vulnerable to disruptive technologies, consider creating a spin-off or smaller group within the company willing to explore these smaller opportunities that are new, unique, and have no comparable equivalent.[28] These groups are then tasked with finding these technologies or innovations and working out the business model that will allow them to take off. From the failure-prevention techniques explored in this book, the best option is to include in your EWS leading indicators, especially in the area of trends and social media discussion among the target market, to provide valuable lead time to either adjust or trigger the preplanned exit strategy.

The next chapter outlines what options are available when failure and underperformance persist. Although there is a mindset opposed to considering and preplanning any kind exit strategy, this same reasoning could be used as an argument for not having an insurance policy, fire alarm, or fire escape plan in your office building. The preplanned exit strategy should be looked at with an open mind. You hope it will never be necessary, but being prepared allows you to either completely turn the situation around or at least survive with some assets left to pursue different opportunities.

6

The Preplanned Exit Strategy

"We are not retreating; we are advancing in another direction."

—General Douglas MacArthur

Despite the high probability of failure or underperformance, most business plans fail to include a trigger point to signal the need for a serious assessment of either a substantially different strategy or an exit strategy. Especially during the honeymoon period of a new venture, the thought of including an exit strategy is, for some, tantamount to "jinxing" the venture, or demonstrates a lack of confidence in the new company or product. The truth, however, is that failing to include a trigger point and preplanned exit strategy is more a sign of negligence than a no-confidence vote. As a previous cruise ship example illustrated, maritime laws mandate lifejackets, rescue boats, and drills not because they know the ship will probably sink (a lack of confidence), but because *not* being prepared for this unlikely, yet nevertheless possible outcome would be criminally negligent.

In business, a preplanned strategy can make the difference between a controlled and minor loss versus losing significant amounts of money, failing to pursue better opportunities, or the possible bankruptcy and closure of the business. Including a trigger point and a preplanned exit strategy in a business plan should become the fifth *P* (product, price, promotion, and placement distribution being the other four) and stand for *pulling out.*

This lack of a pre-established trigger point or preplanned exit strategy is what destroyed investment bank Bear Sterns in 2007. Bear Sterns initially had some $40 million of their own money tied up in two funds made up of complex *collateralized debt obligations* (CDOs) backed by subprime mortgages, which did very well for a number of years. However, once mortgage delinquencies began to climb, the value of CDOs plummeted. Without any trigger point to determine when to stop additional infusions of money to prop up these funds, Bear Sterns ended up pledging some $3 billion by 2007. Fearing that Bear Sterns had a liquidity problem, investors began dumping the stock, precipitating the fire sale of what was once the fifth largest investment bank in the United States.[1] Unfortunately, this has and continues to occur to numerous products and companies. Blockbuster, Circuit City, Sears, K-mart, Polaroid, Iridium, Pets.com, PanAm, Hewlett-Packard's TouchPad, and Barnes and Noble's Nook are all examples of this phenomenon.

The Trigger

Earlier chapters reviewed tools that can prevent or mitigate failure, such as *failure modes and effects analysis* (FMEA), *root cause analysis* (RCA), and the *early warning system* (EWS). Nevertheless, and despite best efforts, there will be failures or nagging underperformance issues that cannot be fixed or that management may decide are not worth the additional time and resources needed to fix them. Therefore, every business should define and establish what conditions should be present so that the trigger point is activated and a preplanned, be it temporary or permanent, exit strategy put into motion.

The reason why it is best to establish the trigger point at an early stage is because once the downturn or crisis occurs, emotions will rule, and more likely than not, more time and money will be spent than would otherwise be necessary. There are two components to the notion of an exit trigger: The trigger itself (which is a signal that you need to go beyond additional remedial efforts), and the preplanned exit strategy. By the time the exit trigger is activated, remedial action should already have taken place, including an RCA of the problem. An exception might be the sudden emergence of a disruptive technology that has doomed your product or market without any advance warning.

The trigger point will vary by company and should be updated periodically as conditions change. The following are some possible baseline criteria to include in your exit or change trigger point:

- **Financial considerations:**
  - — A date by when the venture should break even (e.g., 36 months).
  - — The minimum acceptable return on your investment, and by when it should occur after breakeven (e.g., 5 percent return above the rate of inflation and no later than 12 months after breakeven).
  - — Positive cash flow: If this has been an issue, as it usually tends to be with failing products or businesses, cash flow should be a key metric. After all, it is the one financial metric that cannot be easily distorted or obfuscated by those interested in preserving the status quo. Cash flow targets will vary by company and industry and often by quarter (e.g., retailers and their busy fourth quarter). Figure 6.1 provides an example based on the average free cash flow margin for several industries. Every business should determine its ideal cash flow target margin range based on an analysis of the company needs and market dynamics. As a cautionary note, unless a company has an *activity-based costing* (ABC) system in place, knowing what costs correspond to a specific product (e.g., what percentage of overhead is allocated to that product) will be difficult.

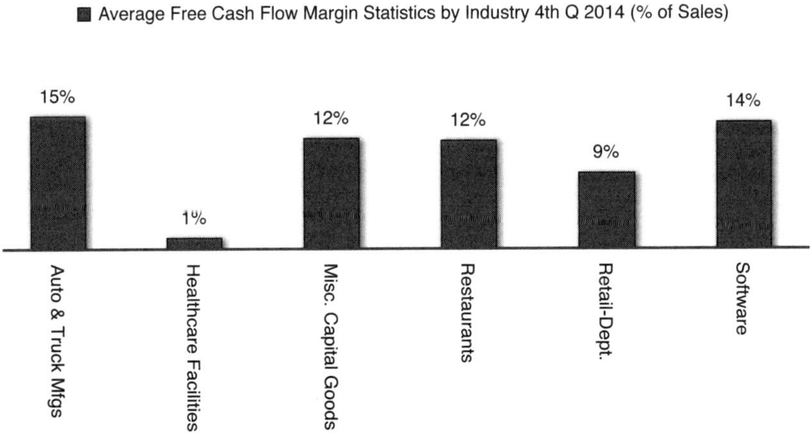

Figure 6.1 Cash flow margin statistics by industry or segment (Source: Based on data from the CSI Market Company)

- **Performance:** Determine what variance from the performance goal is acceptable after remedial action is undertaken (e.g., anything above a 10 percent variance is not acceptable).
- **Market considerations:**
  — What market share needs to be achieved, and within what time period?
  — What is the category growth rate, and are you matching or exceeding it? If you are in a competitive but flat or declining market, staying the course is, in most cases, not a wise choice.
- **On the fence:** If, after considering all these factors, you are still undecided and considering one last rescue attempt, do the following:
  — Confirm that the failure audit was correctly performed on both the initial underperformance and any remedial actions attempted, so that you know exactly what the problem was. Be aware that you are more likely than not falling for the gambler's

fallacy, the mistaken belief that because something negative (a bad result) has occurred frequently in the recent past, that these failures will be less likely to reoccur in the future. Because of this human folly, many people and companies go from losing a few thousand dollars to declaring bankruptcy.

The outlier cases of people and companies that persevered and made it are an example of the survivorship bias effect—because they are so unusual, the media finds them newsworthy, which in turn makes people believe they are more common than they actually are, when in reality they are merely exceptions to the general rule. For every "comeback" story, there are at least 99 cases of companies that lost significantly more money than was necessary.

— Establish an exact figure for what additional time, cost, and effort are reasonable to fix the problem, and if the problem is not resolved after that effort, pursue the exit strategy without further delay.

— Make sure that you are trying remedial actions that are significantly different from previous attempts and which address root cause problems. List those differences and assumptions.

— Decide if there are better opportunities that could be pursued instead of attempting this last rescue attempt. Assign a likelihood of success probability to both the new opportunity and the turnaround of the current venture.

- **Reversibility:** Can you undo your decision before it is fully implemented? Sometimes, though not often, the environment is dynamic, and after the decision is made to drop a product or exit a market, the market changes or a competitor drops out. During this transition period, make sure that you postpone any action that requires a large capital expenditure, especially if that expense is irreversible or not transferable to another product or department within the company.

What Should Never Factor into the Decision

Common reasons for companies and professionals to stay the course despite a low probability of success are the need to protect their reputation, the sunk-cost fallacy, and the gambler's fallacy All of these factors came together in the case of Bear Sterns, which went from a $41 million exposure to billions in losses and its eventual demise. The irony is that if Bear Sterns had limited their exposure to the original $41 million, it would still be around and probably admired for not falling into the trap so many others did.

One should only consider, as hard as it is, the impact of new or additional capital expenditures and forget those made in the past, the sunk costs. We also see the sunk-cost fallacy operating outside of business when victims of domestic violence commonly cite that one reason they stay with their abuser is because of the time and effort they have invested in the relationship; or when countries remain in wars longer than they should, as has occurred throughout history, from the Pyrrhic wars back in 275 B.C. to World War I or, more recently the Vietnam, Iraq, and Afghanistan wars. In all these wars, national prestige, past casualties, and the money spent became anchors and arguments for staying the course, despite the fact that all remedial actions had failed and the probability of a turnaround was highly improbable.

Company, Product, and Market Exits

The focus in this chapter is about exiting a product, service, or business unit rather than closing down the entire company. Closing a company has been covered extensively in numerous books, so there is little "value-add" in repeating that information. Unless stated otherwise, the recommendations here apply to all three situations (product, service, or business unit). Although pioneering work has been done on exit strategies, most prominently by Philip Kotler, this chapter contains additional considerations, the options are structured in a clear manner, and detailed checklists are provided. Figure 6.2 provides a high-level overview of the different types of exit strategies this chapter covers.

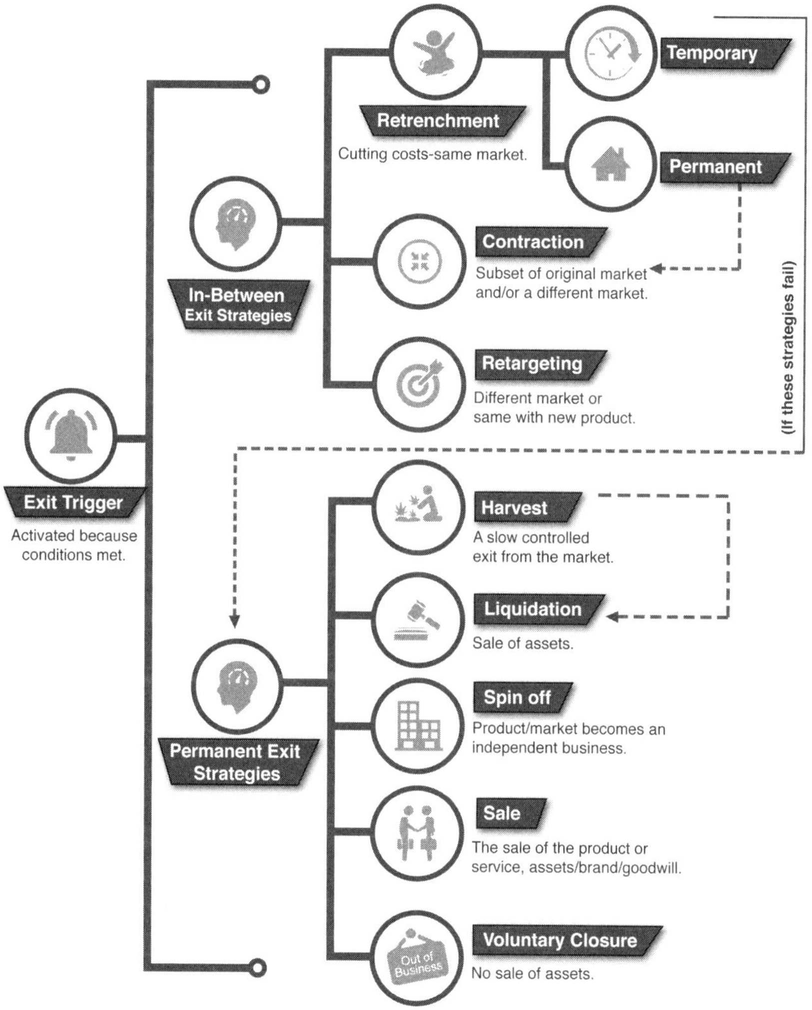

Figure 6.2 Overview of exit strategies

The "In-Between" Strategies (or Plan B)

Before delving into pure exit strategies, there are some "in-between" options shown at the top of Figure 6.2, such as the retrenchment, contraction, and retargeting strategies. The spin-off strategy is a hybrid and could fall under the in-between strategies or the pure exit strategies. However, it is included in the permanent exit grouping because it has closer parallels to the sale (divestment) option. The pure exit strategies entail permanently exiting the product or market, whereas the in-between strategies are an attempt to stay the course, albeit with strategic changes.

These in-between strategies are commonly used by businesses that have some underlying competitive strengths, but lack the means to effectively compete in their current market. The objective in these in-between strategies is to redeploy and concentrate both resources and strengths on either a subset of the current market or an entirely new market where these disadvantages either do not exist or are less pronounced.

Differences Between Retrenchment, Contraction, and Retargeting

A retrenchment strategy, which is often temporary, consists of cutting back on expenses and investments. When a permanent and deeper retrenchment takes place, it usually ends up becoming a contraction strategy. BlackBerry is an example of a retrenchment given that it was forced by circumstances to slash approximately 40 percent of its workforce and drastically reduce its product line. The lack of strategic preplanning is what typically distinguishes a retrenchment from a contraction strategy. Unless BlackBerry pursues a profitable, smaller, and underserved market with differentiated products, its long-term survival is unlikely.

The difference between a *contraction* and a *retargeting* strategy is that in the contraction, the business pursues a smaller target market, be it a subset of the one currently being served or a different market. One of the best-documented cases of a *contraction* strategy was the one pursued by Documentum, a Xerox spin-off, which languished at $2 million in revenue for three years back in the early 1990s. Documentum's strategy during this stagnation period was basically to pursue any Fortune 500 company or department (e.g., R&D, IT, Finance) where they thought their document management software could be used. Fortunately, the company decided to adopt a market segment contraction strategy, shifting its focus to the Regulatory Affairs departments of Fortune 500 pharmaceutical companies. Because there were only 40 of these in the world, the focus and intra-industry word-of-mouth referral effect proved a winning combination. Company revenues jumped to $8 million the following year, then $25 million, $45 million, and $75 million by the fourth year.[2] That is the power of a well-executed and preplanned contraction strategy.

In the *retargeting* strategy, a company pursues a different market of a similar or larger size than the market currently being served. What makes an otherwise neat categorization difficult is that these strategies often evolve and morph. They may start out as a contraction, but then eventually target a new an even larger market or multiple markets. An example of a retargeting strategy occurred in 1924, when Kimberly Clark introduced Kleenex tissues as a substitute for face towels in removing cream and makeup. After languishing for several years and numerous remedial attempts, Kimberly Clark discovered a different target market and usage by offering the tissue as a substitute for the handkerchief. This product-retargeting strategy transformed Kimberly Clark from an industrial paper supplier into a $21 billion consumer goods conglomerate.[3]

Tools for Uncovering Contraction and Retargeting Strategies

Segmentation and positioning are arguably the two most powerful strategic techniques when considering a contraction or retargeting strategy. Most successful alternative strategies pursue a different market segment and also update the positioning statement. A large number of business professionals, when faced with the need for significant remedial action, focus exclusively on tactics such as pricing, product features, promotion, or distribution. These are all parts of the effort needed, but are usually incremental in nature and not *strategic.* It is true that sometimes a tactical element can become a strategy. For example, Dell pursued a direct-to-consumer PC distribution strategy at a time when competitors were only using retailers. However, even in these cases, the tactical element must meet the criteria of good strategy, like meeting one of Porters strategic criteria of either being the lowest cost producer, establishing sufficient differentiation, or adopting a focused strategy (market niche segmentation). After all, what good would Dell's direct distribution strategy have been if its price point were the same as or higher than that of brick-and-mortar retailers?

When deciding which alternative target market segment to pursue, one extremely useful tool is the GE matrix created back in the 1970s by McKinsey for then-client General Electric. See Table 6.1 for an example. Up to that point, the prevailing strategic tool to analyze market attractiveness was the *Boston Consulting Group*'s (BCG) Growth and Market Share matrix (e.g., cows, dogs, stars, and question marks). The BCG tool simplified the analysis down to two factors (growth rate and market share), ignoring equally important variables such as profitability or competitive intensity. Table 6.1 shows an example of two markets being compared using one of the many variations of the GE matrix to help identify the most attractive option.

One should also compare as many scenarios and options as possible. The dimensions analyzed are entirely customizable, and you might want to add dimensions that capture economic, regulatory, or technological factors that play an important role in determining which markets offer your business a better advantage. The number of drivers is also up to the user, but anything fewer than four is probably not enough.

When looking at a contraction or retargeting, seek those market niches where there is less competition, higher growth, or which offer some other significant competitive advantage. Some possible areas to look for niche markets are by location, heavy versus light users, lifetime-value, profitability, underserved customers, and various combinations of these.

Table 6.1 Example of a G.E. Matrix Comparing Two Markets

		Market A		Market B	
	Importance Weight	**Rating**	**Score**	**Rating**	**Score**
Segment target market size	0.25	4	1	2	0.5
Profitability (measured in net profit)	0.25	2	0.5	4	1
Annual growth rate	0.2	2	0.4	4	0.8
Competitive advantage (market penetration)	0.15	2	0.3	4	0.6
Awareness level of our product	0.15	2	0.3	3	0.45
Total (5 would be a perfect score)			**2.5**		**3.35**

A scale would have to be developed for each variable being rated. Here are two rating table examples. One important consideration is that if you use certain types of dimensions, such as competitive intensity; the rating system should reward a lower number or value. For example, a target market with no competition should get a 5 rating, and one with 8 or more competitors should probably get a 1 rating.

Segment Target Market Size	Rating
Less than 100,000	1
100,000–199,999	2
200,000–299,000	3
300,000–499,000	4
500,000 and greater	5

Profitability (Measured in Net Profit)	Rating
Less than 3%	1
Between 3% and 4.9%	2
Between 5% and 7.9%	3
Between 8% and 11.9%	4
More than 12%	5

Many considerations should be addressed before a final decision is made; checklists are provided after each strategy in this chapter. As you evaluate these tasks, you may decide to look at another option and recalibrate your GE matrix if a market proves more costly or difficult to enter than previously anticipated.

Different Scenarios

Complicating matters is the fact that, on some occasions, these strategies may involve the introduction of a completely new product or an altered product.

- A new product being introduced into a completely new market (diversification) is really a new business venture and outside the scope of this exit strategy analysis.
- The introduction of a slightly different but improved product to the same market is, for these purposes, more of a remedial attempt than a retargeting strategy. While the checklist in Table 6.2 can be used in such scenarios, it will not apply to many of the issues encountered.

- Replacing your current product with a completely new product while targeting the same market (e.g., you were selling bikes and now want to sell mopeds) is a form of retargeting. The reason is that even though it is supposedly the same market, your final market may end up being a subset of your original market, if not a completely different market. Therefore, this situation (new product into existing market) does not warrant a separate checklist.

Note about Table 6.2: When determining your timetable, implement those tasks that are reversible first. The reason for this is to avoid alerting customers, vendors, or the competition in case conditions change and you decide to remain in the market. These have been marked with an *R* for reversible and an *I* for irreversible next to each area being evaluated.

Table 6.2 Checklist for a Contraction or Re-targeting Strategy

Areas to Evaluate	Questions and Considerations
Product life cycle (R)	If the product or services focuses on a new market, is the previous product life cycle stage still applicable to your product or category (e.g., perhaps your new target market is entering the maturity stage)?
Awareness level (R)	This is very critical because if in your previous market you had a high level of product awareness and are moving into a market where the awareness level is lower, this will represent a significant challenge and expense that needs to be addressed in the promotional/advertising area through increased spending. (This change could be beneficial if you have a negative perception in the market you are leaving).
Causal forecast drivers, leading indicators, and EWS (R)	As you move into a new market, re-evaluate your assumptions, drivers, leading indicators, and especially the connectors such as the average order size, percentage of repeat customers, frequencies, and so on.
Competition (R)	List the changes in who your primary and potential competitors are; create a grid showing the company and product differences with their strengths and weaknesses, positioning, price point, distribution, and promotions.

Areas to Evaluate	Questions and Considerations
Product	
Number of SKUs or models (I)	Can some of the different models and SKUs be eliminated or phased out?
Features (I)	Can or should some of the existing features be removed? Should new features be added for this target market?
New product replacing current one (I)	Will there be a buyback or credit given for product inventory held by distributors or agents? Incentive to switch: Consider offering existing customers significant incentives to purchase the new product.
Branding (I)	Should the existing brand elements for this (these) new target market(s) be changed?
Process (I)	Will there be any changes to the existing service processes, be it by adding or removing steps or timelines?
Packaging (I)	
Design (I)	Does the current packaging need be redesigned or changed? (focusing on opportunities to cut costs)?
Sizes (I)	If being offered in more than one size or shape, can it be streamlined into fewer options? Will you need a different package size, whether smaller or larger?
Warranty and servicing (R)	Should the current warranty period be extended or reduced? Will any service or repair work policies change?
Administrative employees (I)	Should any positions be eliminated or are new hires needed? Training: Is new training required? Are any employee or management relocations involved?
Sales (I)	Is new training required? Is a reallocation of sales territories needed? Should compensation and bonus structures be changed? The answer should usually be "yes," given the need to align bonuses with potentially more difficult to obtain but profitable business.
Management (R)	Should different managers handle the contraction or retargeting? What retention or compensation techniques might be needed?

Areas to Evaluate	Questions and Considerations
Price (I)	Does the average price need to increase or decrease?
Variable costs (I)	Does the new strategy impact variable costs, and is the effect an increase or decrease? For example, will there be higher or lower freight costs, number of hours of labor required, or loss of volume discounts?
Fixed costs (I)	Are there any opportunities to get rid of equipment or insurance, downsize facilities, relocate to lower-rent facilities, and so on?
Linkages (I)	Will a change in the variable or fixed costs negatively impact any related products in the portfolio? Warning: Unless you use activity-based costing, it will be very difficult to know the impact that one product contraction may have on remaining products in your portfolio.
Discounts/allowances credit or payment terms (R)	Do any of the discounts or allowances offered to customers or distributors need to be added, changed or eliminated?
Advertising and promotions (R)	What updates or changes need to be made to any of the following: Collateral Promotions Advertising Public relations Promotions Digital search, mobile, social media
Company-owned stores (I)	Do the number and type of outlets need to be increased or decreased?
Distribution type and reach (both R and I)	Do you need to change or add distribution strategy, whether direct, indirect, or a mix? Will distribution reach increase, decrease, or stay the same?
Channel partners (I)	Do you need to add or eliminate existing distributors or agents? Consider whether your reach is not impacted by pruning your distributors as long as performance minimums are met by the remaining ones. The reason is that by granting an exclusive, the remaining distributors should see an increase in volume and margins and therefore be more likely to promote your product (e.g., if you now sell through two bike shops in Atlanta versus the previous ten outlets, the remaining two shops should see less competitive price pressure and therefore want to promote you over other brands available in the eight other locations).

Areas to Evaluate	Questions and Considerations
Geographic changes (both R and I)	Will the new focus mean a shift to different geographic areas? If so, what are the implications in terms of employees and resources
Inventory levels (R)	Do you need to change current inventory levels and policies?
SGA (R)	Are there any opportunities to cut costs in any and each of the selling, general, and administrative areas?
R&D (both R and I)	Do you need to invest in new or different R&D areas, or can some of costs be cut?
Positioning (I)	As you went through the list, there were probably changes in several areas such as distribution, pricing, customer base, product features, services, packaging, or geography. See whether those changes offer new differentiation opportunities. Is the current positioning still relevant for the new market or subset of the current target market? Re-evaluate whether your competitors changed.
Timeline and implementation	Because every task has been categorized as either reversible or irreversible, whenever possible place the "reversible" decisions at the beginning of your implementation plan and leave the irreversible ones to the end. The reason is that if the situation changes, such as a competitor exiting before you, or the new market you were going to target plummets, you may be able to reverse course.
Communication plan (I)	Decide how and when this would be communicated to the different stakeholders. Ideally, nothing should be mentioned until you start to get into the irreversible changes.

Exit Strategies

What follows is a discussion of pure exit strategies—those undertaken when your company decides to permanently abandon a product, service, or market. This occurs when either all remedial attempts (tactical or strategic) have failed, or management has decided because of the low probability of success or unfavorable payback that it is not worth staying the course. There are several different approaches one can take, as the overview in Figure 6.2 illustrated.

The Psychology of the Exit Decision

> *"Being alert to the possible negatives in any situation is the best way to bring about positive results."*
>
> —Bob Knight, Hall of Fame Basketball coach and author of *The Power of Negative Thinking*

An ingrained belief in our media-hyped entrepreneurial folklore is that failure is not an option and that all successful visionaries who may have struggled with failure eventually succeeded through sheer willpower. This is an overly simplistic conclusion based on a few cherry picked examples and ignores the fact that according to the U.S. Bureau of Labor, 75 percent of new businesses are not around 15 years later. Moreover, 50 percent of these closures occur during the fifth year of business, indicating willpower was probably not the issue, given that most were probably trying to remedy problems throughout that period. Is the high rate of business failure and underperformance due to a lack of willpower or to weak ideas, poor execution, bad timing, failure to learn from mistakes, or insufficient cash? Cash, unlike willpower, is a finite resource, not usually available in abundance. Squander it and you are essentially out of the game. This problem is not limited to business. Many young people spend an inordinate amount of time on sports versus academics hoping to become a professional player. A hard look at the success statistics of professional sports should make parents think twice. After all, only .03% of high school basketball players ever make it the *National Basketball League* (NBA).

The idea of having a preplanned exit strategy is not based on emotion but rather on the statistics of failure. The trigger point assumes that remedial attempts have been attempted but the probability of future success still remains low. The question, especially for the not-so-young entrepreneurs, is this: Do you want to exit early or drag it out a few more years, thereby probably physically and emotionally exhausting yourself, not to mention spending all your savings? This isn't to say everyone should give up permanently, but by exiting intelligently you may be able to fight another day on a better playing field, much as General MacArthur did. The Japanese Kamikaze approach, while fearsome and brave (or lunacy, depending on your viewpoint), was from a military perspective not very effective in changing the course of any battle.

That being said, there are some businessmen, especially entrepreneurs, who should after one or several failures consider completely giving up and focusing on safer and more realistic opportunities or at the very least finding more business savvy partners. Because unless you have a technical or scientific breakthrough, the odds are very much stacked against you after a failure or continued underperformance.

The Harvesting Strategy: The Slow Exit

In the *harvesting* strategy, your objective is to leave the market slowly, losing market share in exchange for an improvement in profits and cash flow by cutting expenses and investments. This strategy, however, is the riskiest and most difficult to implement given that, to be successful, it must be kept secret from most of your employees, competitors, customers, and vendors. Kotler has suggested the following conditions be present when deciding on a harvesting strategy:[4]

- You are in a stable or declining market with low to average profits.
- You have either a small market share or one that is becoming difficult to defend or maintain.
- The product is not strategically important to your business.
- Attempts to improve your market share have proven futile.
- Your opportunity costs are significant.
- There is no contribution to the overall business portfolio product.

The Risky Strategy

For a harvesting strategy to be successful, it must be conducted in a stealthy manner so that nobody knows you are planning to eventually exit the market. If the market finds out, the consequences can be a precipitous and fatal collapse of your business. Depending on what you sell, customers may not want to risk being unable to get parts or support, and those in your distribution channel may want to avoid carrying inventory that may soon be obsolete. Moreover, competitors will probably spread rumors and launch aggressive customer acquisition campaigns. This is what happened to General Motors in November 1992 when a false rumor circulated that GM would be phasing out the Oldsmobile brand. A month after the rumor started, sales fell by one-third compared to the previous month.[5]

In a harvest strategy, you are always trying to cut costs across the board: R&D, SG&A, materials, processes, bonuses, fixed costs, services, and so on. However, proceed with caution if you are in a high-liability industry, such as food products, healthcare, or chemicals, where cost cutting could adversely impact the products' safety or efficacy, resulting in injury or death. A case has been made that the toxic leak in Bhopal, India, in 1984 (which killed more than 5,000 people), was a direct consequence of a harvesting strategy being implemented by Union Carbide.[6]

To minimize the downside of a harvesting strategy gone wrong, consider implementing this strategy only in low-liability, mature markets with relatively low growth rates and above-average prices. The reason for this is because you will have a better chance of recovering under those circumstances should rumors about your exit start circulating. You can perhaps lower your price to remain viable or, if in a mature market, go ahead and accelerate your exit timetable. Exiting sooner than planned in a mature market would not be as detrimental as being forced to exit during a growth stage when you had been planning to stay until the maturity stage. Table 6.3 provides a checklist of questions and considerations you should make before proceeding with a harvest strategy

Note for Table 6.3: When determining your timetable, place those tasks that are reversible first. The reason for this is to avoid alerting customers, vendors, or the competition in case conditions change and you decide to remain in the market. They have been labeled as *R* for reversible and *I* for irreversible next to each area being evaluated.

Table 6.3 Harvesting Checklist

Areas to Evaluate	Questions and Considerations
Impact on other brands	Will there be any negative issues or repercussions on any of the remaining brands, including the company?
Causal forecast drivers, leading indicators and EWS	As you begin decelerating your activities, do you need to adjust your drivers, leading indicators, and especially connector assumptions (e.g., average order size, percentage of repeat customers, frequencies). Because the objective is to improve cash flow and profits, you need to maintain a reasonable level of revenue.
Customers	Are they dependent on this product (e.g., medicine), and are there any substitutes? Are there any contractual agreements with a customer preventing an exit? Can credit procedures be tightened to improve cash flow?
Competition	Identify the competitor who is the most likely to benefit from any leak and minimize any contacts and signals.
Product Changes	
Number of SKUs or models	Of the different models and SKUs, can some be phased out before others?
Features (I)	Can some of the existing features be removed earlier?
Packaging and design (R)	Can costs be cut in packaging or design?
Sizes (R)	If offered in more than one size, can they be streamlined into fewer options?

Areas to Evaluate	Questions and Considerations
Warranty and servicing	
Warranties (R)	Can the current warranty period be shortened? How will warranties be honored after the exit?
Servicing (R)	Will any service or repair work policies change?
Services	
Process (I)	Will there be any changes to existing service processes, whether removing steps or changing timelines?
People (I)	Do you need to eliminate positions? If so, by when? Who?
Physical evidence (I)	Are there any changes needed to facilities, whether offices or retail locations? Can you move to lower-rent locations depending on the time frame?
Price	
Price (R)	Can the price be increased and if so by what percentage?
Variable costs	Will the eventual market share decline result in an increase in variable costs due to any lost volume discounts?
Fixed costs	Any opportunities, early on, to get rid of equipment, insurance, tax benefits, downsize facilities, etc.?
Linkages (I)	Will a change in variable or fixed costs negatively impact any related products that will continue?
Discounts/allowances credit or payment terms (R)	Can any of the discounts or allowances offered to customers or distributors be reduced or eliminated?
Advertising and promotions (both R and I)	Decide what can be eliminated and what needs to remain so the decline is not too precipitous: Collateral Promotions Advertising Personal selling Public relations Promotions Digital search, mobile, social media

Areas to Evaluate	Questions and Considerations
Placement-Distribution	
Company stores or outlets (I)	Can the number or type of outlets be reduced or downsized?
Channel partners (I)	Can some distributors or agents be dropped where margins are not as good? Are there any contracts that renew automatically? Gather all your deadlines to make sure that they do not automatically rollover.
Distribution reach (R)	What minimum distribution reach is needed during the harvest period?
Inventory levels (R)	Can current inventory levels be reduced?
SGA (R)	Any opportunities to cut costs in each of the selling, general, and administrative expense areas?
R&D (both R and I)	By what percentage can R&D investments be decreased?
Timeline and communication plan	Develop a timeline and plan to implement when each of the above must occur. Decide how and when this would be communicated to the different stakeholders.
Sale of remaining assets (I)	When the product or market is finally abandoned, see liquidation checklist.

Faster Exit Strategies

The remaining options involve faster—at least in theory—exit strategies. These consist of the sale of the product or service, a spin-off, liquidation, or voluntary closure. In the sale and spin-off options, there are some opportunities to extract additional value above that of the remaining assets. These types of exit strategies are usually driven by the following:

- The existence of factors that prevent a harvest strategy (e.g., high liability or probability of being discovered)
- The existence of better opportunities

- A rapid deterioration in the market (e.g., the emergence of a disruptive technology)
- A good selling opportunity with a qualified buyer

With the exception of the spin-off, potential downsides to these exit strategies include the following:

- A possible miscalculation of the impact the closure may have on other parts of your portfolio (e.g., shared overhead costs)
- Overlooked or unforeseen liabilities (e.g., outstanding warranties or other contractual issues, such as employment contracts)
- Tax consequences
- The potential of strengthening a competitor of the remaining or future areas of your business

The Spin-Off

If the product or service you want to exit is substantial enough in terms of revenue or value, a spin-off should be a top consideration. Because of the legal and operational complexities involved in a spin-off and lack of a cash infusion, the spin-off is usually not an option for cash-strapped or smaller companies.

The spin-off is also a great way to minimize the risk of empowering competitors, getting hit by capital gains taxes, or not finding a buyer within a reasonable time frame. If there are no buyers and you remain in a state of limbo and the competitive environment deteriorates, it could further damage your ability to sell your business at a profit. In the spin-off, the product or services and all the assets (patents, inventory, accounts receivable) and liabilities (accounts payable, liens) associated with them are folded into a new, independent business. If shares are involved, the stockholders in the original business receive equivalent shares in the new company to compensate for the fact that some value was extracted from the original company.

Very often, management in the new business will take a pay cut in exchange for equity, improving the cash flow and management focus. As an added bonus, there are usually no tax consequences because no income was earned by the split. This is a different situation from a sale, where there will usually be some appreciation that took place over time that could trigger a hefty and unexpected capital gains tax bill. A checklist for the spin off has been combined with that of the sales (given their similarities) in Table 6.4.

The Sale

In this scenario, you are selling the product, service, or business unit to another company. As in any exit strategy, it is best to keep the decision confidential and on a need-to-know basis. The reason being that it may take months to find a buyer, and if it were to become public knowledge, some of the same negative market dynamics present, as when a harvest strategy becomes known, may adversely impact you. (See Table 6.4 for a checklist of things to consider.) As long as the process is done discreetly (e.g., through a broker that anonymizes your company information, contacts a preapproved list of prospects, and requires confidentiality agreements), it is unlikely that customers, vendors, or competitors will find out. With a sale or spin-off, the usual cost cutting is not present; it should essentially be business as usual.

Table 6.4 Checklist for the Sale or Spin-Off

Areas to Evaluate	Questions and Considerations
Impact on other brands	Will there be any negative issues or repercussions on the remaining brands, including the company brand?
Product linkages	Will the loss of volume negatively impact any remaining products?
Company-owned stores or outlets	Are there contractual agreements or leases? When do they end or what is the buyout amount?
Channel partners	What agreement if any is there with the channel such as an exclusive or the need to provide notice around inventory buybacks?

Areas to Evaluate	Questions and Considerations
Assets included	Are the following included in the sale, or will they be absorbed by the remaining business? Accounts receivable included Inventory Real estate Manufacturing equipment Licensing Patents Trademarks
Liabilities	Pending or potential litigation. Environmental cleanup. Accounts payable included in the sale? Non-sellable inventory. Make sure all representations are accurate. Bad debts.
Roadblocks	Detailed listing of agreements with banks, creditors, vendors, distributors or employees. Make sure that any deadlines for notices are observed.
Employees	Notifications: Will some employees be terminated before the sale/spin-off? Severance: How and who determines it? Retention and bonuses agreements to maintain the business.
Tax	What are the tax implications of the spin-off or sale?
Timeline and communication plan	Develop a timeline and a plan to implement when each of the above tasks must occur. Decide how and when this would be communicated to the different stakeholders.
Additional tips on preparing for a sale	Partial seller financing: This option could make the tax implications less onerous and may even allow you to stay in business as a minority partner. To weaken a competitor, consider approaching their competitors as well. They may like the opportunity and have more resources than you to neutralize or at least keep them busy.

Liquidation and Voluntary Closure

The remaining two options are very similar, except that in the liquidation, you are attempting to sell some of the remaining assets, whereas in the voluntary closure option, you redeploy those assets to another business line or dispose of them (e.g., donate or discard). Table 6.5 is a detailed checklist of considerations and questions that should be asked. These exit strategies tend to happen for the following reasons:

- **The liquidation:** The exit was delayed too much or the debacle very sudden (e.g., Bear Sterns), leaving little to no value in your product or business. As a result, the sale or spin-off is no longer a viable option.
- **The voluntary closure:** This can be the same scenario as in the liquidation but with no buyer or assets to sell. In some cases, a company might not want to create or embolden competitors, so it may decide not to sell any of its assets or the business unit. One company that is known to do this is ADM (Archer Daniels Midland). When they close a seed oil refining facility, for example, they would rather sell the machinery as scrap than sell the equipment whole and possibly strengthen an existing competitor or encourage someone else to enter the market.

Table 6.5 Checklist for the Liquidation or Voluntary Closure

Areas to Evaluate	Questions and Considerations
Impact on other brands	Will there be any negative issues or repercussions on remaining brands, including the company brand?
Customers	Are they dependent on this product (e.g., medicine)? Are there substitutes? Is there any agreement preventing an exit?
Warranty and servicing	Make sure that warranties and service guarantee responsibilities are either transferred or terminated legally.
Product linkages	Will the sale and loss of volume or other discounts negatively impact any remaining products?

Areas to Evaluate	Questions and Considerations
Company-owned stores or outlets	Are there contractual agreements or leases? When do they end or what is the buyout amount?
Channel partners	What agreement if any is there with the channel such as an exclusive or the need to provide notice around inventory buybacks?
Assets included	Which of the following is included in the sale or will they be absorbed by the remaining business? Accounts receivable to be included Inventory Real estate Manufacturing equipment Licensing Patents Trademarks
Liabilities	Pending or potential litigation. Environmental cleanup. Accounts payable included in the sale? Non-sellable inventory. Make sure all representations are accurate. Bad debts.
Net (assets and liabilities)	Are there enough assets to cover the liabilities? If not, the question of declaring bankruptcy or setting up a payment plan with debtors needs to be addressed.
Roadblocks	Listing of all the agreements if any with banks, creditors, vendors, distributors or employees. Make sure that any deadlines for notices are observed.
Employees	Severance, notice; health insurance, vacation, bonuses, stock options.
Tax	Are there any tax implications in the sale of assets?
Timeline and communication plan	Develop a timeline and plan to implement when each of the above must occur; decide how and when this would be communicated to the different stakeholders.

The preplanned exit strategy concept should be seen as a living document; the choice you initially made may need to be revisited if the trigger event occurs several years later; by then both your company and the marketplace will have experienced significant changes. For example, if you decided on a sales exit strategy but were only in the marketplace for a year, you will more likely than not have to do a liquidation or voluntary closure. A completely different situation occurs if you have been in business for five or more years; you might be able to sell the product, service, or business and get additional money beyond your assets (e.g., goodwill). Finally, having a preplanned exit strategy in place should be psychologically comforting and reduce the stress level; the feeling of being in control is what prevents hasty and panicked decision-making when things go wrong.

Epilogue

Challenges with Domain Transfers and the Next Major Domain Transfer

One of my objectives in putting together this book was to make sure the material was both practical and actionable. I steered clear of complex, expensive solutions and software. All the techniques presented have and are being used by millions of professionals around the world. None of them require any capital expenditures or special skills, and many can be accomplished using a simple spreadsheet. Techniques such as the *early warning system* (EWS) or setting up an exit trigger will only take a few hours of time, while the *failure mode and effects analysis* (FMEA), failure audit using *root cause analysis* (RCA), and the preplanned exit strategy techniques may take a day—or a few days at most.

Facilitating Adoption

Nevertheless, the obstacles that might prevent most people from adopting domain transfers of failure-prevention or mitigation techniques are the lack of time and various mental blocks. For small businesses, there might also be some trepidation and/or a perceived lack of knowledge about being able to implement these techniques; for those cases, I suggest that just challenging your frameworks, creating an EWS, exit trigger, and attempting a basic failure audit using RCA are all low-hanging fruit that require only a few hours of your time. Moreover, the time invested in these techniques is never a waste because you have to ask questions and analyze initiatives to find explanations for past problems.

Larger companies with ample resources should institutionalize the failure analysis techniques covered in this book into areas that have never used them, including marketing, sales, finance, product management, and strategic planning. Without adequate failure-mitigation techniques, companies run the risk of engaging in ill-conceived new initiatives. Unless the root causes of any current underperformance are known, there is a good chance of carrying over the same underlying deficiencies to new ventures.

Finding the Team Leader

The two skills professionals need to successfully implement these techniques in a large and complex organization or business are *domain knowledge expertise* and being *process savvy.* Unfortunately, in many of the disciplines needing these techniques the most (strategy, marketing, finance, and sales), process skills are often both lacking and even disliked. Outsourcing the task to a process group, such as supply chain or operations, is not a good solution because they probably lack the necessary domain expertise. For example, a supply chain professional trying to solve a finance or sales failure would waste time asking basic or irrelevant questions while at the same time failing to ask the deeper, more probing questions needed.

Moreover, many failure analysis techniques such as FMEA and RCA require a team effort in large organizations. This entails finding a team leader to manage and correctly implement the techniques. One potential pool of candidates to lead this effort may be found in the analytics group, a growing area in most companies. Analysts tend to specialize in functional areas within the company, with some supporting sales, others marketing, and others focusing on strategy or finance. These professionals tend to be process oriented because many analytical tasks require following a certain process or protocol. Some amount of additional training would still be required, but their process orientation, quantitative focus, and decent domain expertise are all major advantages. An added benefit in recruiting from the analytics group is their objectivity. Because failure analysis and assigning responsibilities carries negative connotations, it is unrealistic to expect any person representing the group responsible for the failure to maintain the necessary objectivity. Regardless of which team leader is chosen, support from upper management is vital. Without it, both the team and team leader will be subject to potential intimidation or retaliation by the affected people or departments.

Triggers, Protocols, and Documentation

In addition to finding and training the right person to lead these techniques, it is also important to establish the triggers to determine what underperformance or failure warrants an RCA or FMEA. Is an underperformance variance of 10 percent the trigger? What monetary amount at play in a new campaign warrants a FMEA? Is it anything over $5,000, or is $50,000 the target? Note that all mission-critical tasks such as the launch of a new product or its failure should always trigger the use of FMEA and RCA.

Another component in formalizing and institutionalizing failure prevention and mitigation is to establish teams by functional area, such as sales, marketing, finance, strategy, and so on. It is important to predesignate who will be participating on the team so that the team leader can train those individuals on the basic tenets of these techniques. For example, to conduct an RCA for a failed sales campaign, representatives from sales, marketing, market research and analytics areas, and possibly operations and customer service should be included.

Incentivizing Behaviors

The stigma associated with failure and the desire to move on after it occurs is a powerful force. Our survival instincts make us not want to dwell on the negative. However, those same survival instincts also demand we learn from failure; otherwise, we risk repeating it. So in addition to formalizing and institutionalizing failure analysis techniques, it is important that a company reward the desired behaviors and outcomes. One sure-fire way to make the implementation and cooperation of these studies and analyses successful is to make them a component of the employee review process and, if applicable, a part of any bonuses. This will reduce the inevitable resistance that occurs when someone is being asked for an explanation or is held accountable for their underperformance or failure. Moreover, when such efforts are being implemented for the first time, it is important not to punish employees unless there is malfeasance or if previously uncovered issues are not corrected.

Professional Certifications

An additional problem for many business disciplines is the lack of any mandated professional proficiency certification. Law, accounting, and medicine all have professional licensing requirements, and although they do not guarantee brilliance, they do provide some proof of baseline competency. The exams are also rigorous enough so that some do not pass on their first attempt. In law, some 36 percent fail the bar exam,[1] in medicine 8 percent fail the general practitioner exam,[2] and some 50 percent fail the Certified Public Accountants exam.[3] There are some individuals who struggle and retake the exam numerous times, and some never pass even after multiple attempts, which is a good thing. For example, in medicine, of those who have to repeat the exam, 45 percent fail again. If there were no medical licensing requirements, one might be treated by someone so incompetent that they lack the most basic medical knowledge.

Because recent college graduates must pass these exams to practice their professions, colleges and universities design and improve their programs so that their graduates are successful. It also creates uniformity in subject matter among the various educational and training programs. Another benefit is that professionals in these fields are required to remain current with new technologies or emerging topics through ongoing professional education requirements. For example, Certified Public Accountants in Texas need to take 120 hours of continuing professional education in each 3-year reporting period with a minimum of 20 hours in each 1-year period.

There are many non-mandatory certifications for different business disciplines, but they all face the following problems:

- They are not mandatory and often not as rigorous as mandatory professional certifications, with the exception of some finance certifications.
- Industry is for the most part unaware of many of the certifications, and rarely asks for them unless it is in highly specialized areas such as Google AdWords for digital advertising, or a SAS certification for data analytics.
- There are no continuing education requirements.
- Higher education has low awareness of these certifications and as a result has not adjusted curriculums to meet a national standard. As a result, someone could have a marketing degree and still not understand segmentation, or claim an advertising degree without understanding emerging media buying platforms such as programmatic buying, or a professional salesperson who does not know how to effectively use a *customer relationship management* (CRM) tool, or a finance major who cannot read a cash flow statement. This is akin to a physician not knowing key human physiological concepts.

An Unlikely but Potential Solution

State governments will probably never require mandatory certifications for finance, product management, marketing, strategy or professional sales. Finance, however, is one discipline that has done an admirable job with its Charted Financial Analyst and Certified Financial Planner certifications. Given that a state mandate would not make much sense for these professions, the more realistic option is to follow the path of the financial certifications. To get traction, Fortune 500 companies, agencies, colleges, and professional organizations would need to come together and create a rigorous certification program. The key would be if major employers, agencies, and Fortune 500 companies started giving preference to job applicants holding the certification, with the ultimate goal of requiring it. Initially, it would probably be better to start by requiring current and more junior employees in these fields to take the new certification to identify and address knowledge deficiencies and make them maintain their proficiency through the required continuing education.

The Future Domain Transfer: Artificial Intelligence

Artificial intelligence (AI) is a subjective and broad term that usually entails the ability of a machine to replicate the cognitive functions of a human. However, because humans also possess common sense as well as irrational, intuitive, and emotional behaviors, the jury is still out on whether AI will be able to mimic humans any time in the near or even distant future. Although the term *cognitive computing* might be more appropriate than AI, the reality is that the term AI has made its way into mainstream media and the public's consciousness, so that is the term used in this chapter.

As AI enters the introductory stages of adoption, along with opportunities, it is also creating a good deal of angst. Famous scientific and technology luminaries such as Stephen Hawking, Elon Musk, Steve Wozniak, and Bill Gates have warned about AI's potential to become an existential danger to humans, through cybercrime, hacking of vital infrastructure, financial trading run amok between battling AI systems, or rogue AI systems overriding human commands. Others bring up AI's potential to eliminate large swaths of jobs in customer service, professional drivers (e.g., taxicabs, trucks), writers, and even professional jobs such as accounting, finance, marketing, and supply chain. How quickly this happens and to what extent is dependent on the ability of AI to better mimic human intelligence.

Code-breaker and mathematician Alan Turing introduced the *Turing test* as a kind of litmus test to determine when a machine possessed intelligence equal to or at least indistinguishable from that of a human. In the test, a remote and text-only interaction between a machine and a human takes place on one end; the AI machine and human each take turns answering questions from a panel of judges. If the AI machine can fool the judges at least 30 percent of the time during a five-minute interval, the machine has passed the Turing test. In 2014, a Russian program called Eugene, portraying itself as a 13-year-old Ukrainian boy to explain away its broken English, fooled 33 percent of the judges after five minutes of questioning.[4] While 33 percent may seem somewhat low, the advances in AI that have been made to date are enough to provide useful value in many areas with even smarter virtual assistants than Siri or Cortana.

How Artificial Intelligence Works

The concept of AI has been around since the late 1950s, and as with any emerging technology, there have been ups and downs, along with good doses of hype and overreach. However, recent improvements, scalability potential, and current business use cases seem to all indicate that technology is moving into a phase as transformational, if not more so than when the Internet was introduced to consumers in the early 1990s.

We have all seen examples of components of AI in action, whether Apple's Siri, Microsoft's Cortana, and most notably IBM's Watson. In 2011, Watson took on two of the most successful *Jeopardy* champions, one of whom was unbeaten during his previous 74 appearances. By the end of the competition, Watson defeated both players and accumulated $77,000 in winnings, leaving the second-place champion far behind with only $24,000. This *Jeopardy* breakthrough was much more complex than when Big Blue beat the reigning chess champion, Gary Kasparov, a few years earlier. The chess challenge, while complex, was more aligned with cognitive computing strengths such as memorizing how each piece moves, a clear final objective (checkmating the King), and anticipating and optimizing its next move as much as 40 steps ahead in the match.

For the *Jeopardy* contest, Watson was "trained" (machine learning) over a three-year period by providing it with thousands of past trivia questions and the correct answer for each. Watson's algorithms then analyzed and identified patterns, identifying what information it needed to correctly answer those questions. To determine whether Watson had learned the subject matter, it was then asked new questions. If these new questions were answered incorrectly, the correct answer was provided so that the machine could learn from its mistakes. In essence, AI is learning from failure, discerning what matters and what does not, and also what the varying importance of different elements (weights) are to arrive at the correct answer.

The *Jeopardy* display was not only remarkable because Watson could understand natural language (e.g., that the '40s meant the 1940s and not the 1840s or something else) or access staggering volumes of information and yet provide an answer within three seconds (e.g., it had been fed some 200 million pages of information), but also because before answering a question, Watson would assess how sure it was that it knew the correct answer and refrain from answering unless a confidence threshold of at least 80 percent was met. If that confidence threshold was not achieved, it would go through the machine learning process again after hearing the correct answer.[5]

This kind of self-control and discipline are essential in failure prevention. The following two key elements were at work in the *Jeopardy* example:

- A high degree of confidence in the accuracy of both the answer and the information used to arrive at that conclusion (answering a question in this example)
- The introspection to go back and determine what process or information it *should* have used to arrive at the correct answer

One apparent downside was that for the *Jeopardy* challenge, Watson required 90 servers, 16 terabytes of memory, and 4 terabytes of clustered storage. Fortunately, in a matter of just a few years, Watson now requires 90 percent less hardware and memory to handle similar tasks. In addition, there is promising work on a new type of processor called a *neuromorphic chip.* To make a long story short, these new chips operate more like our brain, processing millions of instructions in parallel and at lightning speed.[6] Also, most if not all commercial AI systems will probably continue to be made available as cloud-based services, making the infrastructure issue a moot point. However, and as might be expected, there are storage and energy costs associated with running these types of systems, which have to be absorbed by the end user somehow, somewhere.

A bigger challenge hindering faster adoption of AI is that the "machine learning" effort can be substantial. It can take months to teach a system a new and complex business area. One possible solution is an advanced type of machine learning called *deep learning,* in which both IBM and Google are investing considerable resources. Deep learning (advanced neural network) algorithms *reduce* but do not eliminate the amount of training, data, or subsequent calibration efforts required. Reducing this setup time would greatly accelerate the adoption process by minimizing the human effort currently required to train an AI system. One example of deep learning's potential was put on display when an AI system learned to play an Atari video game largely on its own, improving in a matter of hours to the point that it was soon playing at a level no human could match, including novel ways to win.[7] The limitations of a deep learning system and whether it can be as effective in complicated domains such as medicine or business remain to be seen. Figure E.1 provides an overview of the different components of artificial intelligence.

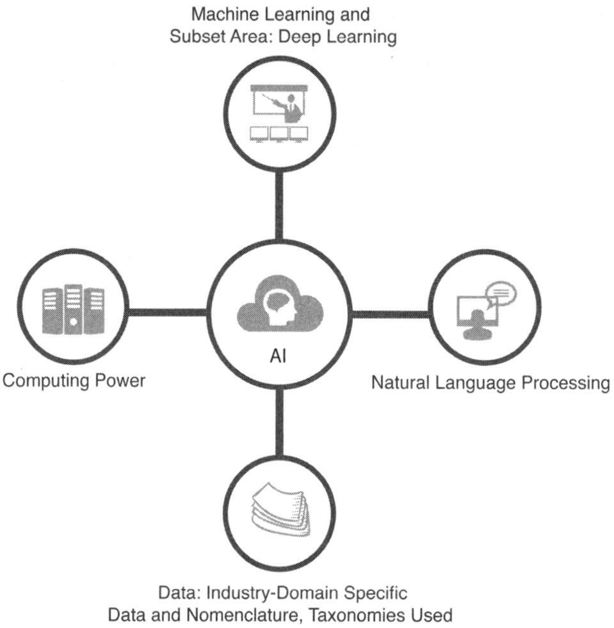

Figure E.1 Components of artificial intelligence

Artificial Intelligence Players

In addition to IBM, there is a multitude of both large and relatively unknown start-ups offering a variety of AI flavors for different purposes. The usual players like Google, Microsoft, and the Chinese search giant Baidu are all prioritizing and pouring billions into the field of AI both within their companies and by investing in start-ups. Apple, at least so far, does not appear as active as one might expect, although they are hiring in this area and probably hedging their bets as they did with mobile payments, jumping in once the better technology and approach begins to dominate and the kinks are worked out. Facebook and Amazon are also actively investing in start-ups such as Vicarious, which aims to leverage AI for aggregating and providing answers (crowdsourcing) from Facebook or Amazon's user base, applying facial recognition to videos and images, and intelligent image recognition. In the image-recognition area, Vicarious was able to "imagine" new positions and orientations even though it had never seen the original image shape or contour before. By applying this algorithm, Vicarious was able to figure out the CAPTCHA images seen on website forms (the ones designed to prevent malware or spam software from bypassing and filling out these forms).[8] Facebook is developing a method it calls *Pose Invariant PErson Recognition* (PIPER), which allows its algorithm to recognize a person with an 80+ percent accuracy rate by looking at a person from the side or back despite only having a frontal picture to work from.[9] This is facial recognition taken to the next level. This software can recognize people in crowds or stores for that matter; the implications are numerous, such as Facebook being able to demonstrate to a retailer how effective Facebook ads are in driving people to the store, where their images are captured by CCTV. These breakthroughs are bringing AI closer to mimicking humans, especially as AI and robotics combine.

As for Google, most of their efforts reside in the secretive Google X research lab in a project called *Google Brain.* Google is probably leveraging AI throughout its many properties, whether Google Maps, Android Voice, Search, Shopping, and maybe even pesky areas such as advertising fraud. In addition to bolstering its internal resources, Google is buying and investing in start-ups like Deep Mind, a London-based start-up with the world's largest team of researchers specializing in deep learning.[10]

Walled Garden Ecosystem Versus "Democratized" Artificial Intelligence

AI is clearly a competitive advantage to many of these large players, and while its use will benefit their users through better search results, smarter virtual assistants, or self-driving cars, their AI technology is not something other companies will be able to leverage for their specific needs. These large players are for the most part taking a walled-off, insular approach to AI by not granting access to third parties.

One notable exception among the large players is IBM, which is making available different types of "AI" components to businesses, some at no cost, like the natural language processing data analysis tool Watson Analytics (without the machine learning component), or its deep learning tool Alchemy API, which can be used by developers to create AI-powered mobile apps using a freemium or a paid pricing model, depending on usage. In addition, IBM has set aside more than a $100 million for investments in start-ups that use Watson. Recently, $100,000 in seed money was awarded to a team of students from the University of Texas at Austin. The students won an IBM competition by developing an AI smartphone app designed to help Texas residents find information about healthcare, food assistance, and other social services in partnership with the United Way in Austin.[11] In addition to the large players, there are a growing number of start-ups in the AI space offering AI tools and services for businesses; however, it is still too early to know which ones will survive or offer scalable and easy-to-use systems.

Failure and Artificial Intelligence

AI has a great future in failure mitigation and prevention even though it is not currently being positioned or talked about in that context. In healthcare, for example, researchers at Indiana University compared the performance of physician and patient outcomes against the performance of an AI-driven model and its patient outcomes. The artificial intelligence-based model obtained a 30 percent to 35 percent increase in positive patient outcomes or, to put it another way, the AI solution reduced poor outcomes (failure or underperformance) by 30 percent to 35 percent.[12]

Companies that start institutionalizing failure analysis techniques such as FMEA and RCA, in addition to reaping benefits today, will have a significant advantage as AI becomes more pervasive. The reason is that they will have the relevant body of data available that is so critical for the "machine learning" component of AI. Once the machine learns the causes and patterns of past failures, it can provide feedback on the probability of success or failure for future ventures specific to that vertical or industry. As a bonus with AI, one can add data that may not have originally been a part of the FMEA or RCA (e.g., social media, weather, customer complaints, returns) but which may yield interesting insights that can then be included in future FMEAs or EWSs.

IBM Watson's Chief Technology Officer, Rob High, shared his take on the possible use of AI (*cognitive computing* is his preferred terminology) to some of the failure techniques covered in this book. AI is most useful for the inductive FMEA technique, given its similarity to current uses of AI in the medical diagnosis and oncology research field. When conducting an FMEA, there are many possible causes and assumptions that must be identified, and which are difficult to do when being done *a priori.* As in the chess example, once the AI system has been taught using past FMEAs and the data that supported them, future FMEAs can be built and improved by closing any gaps, recalibrating weights, and foreseeing many other possible outcomes. Other low-hanging fruit include the EWS, given AI's potential to find additional leading indicators to help identify possible underperformance even earlier. As discussed in previous chapters, there is the ever-present challenge of being able to distinguish cause-effect relationships from random coincidences that often occur with large data sets. In a matter of seconds or minutes, AI can conduct dozens or even hundreds of experiments using time series data to validate whether there is, in fact, a true cause-effect relationship so that you can make evidence-based and reliable recommendations.

A related example from medicine shows how AI can help in reducing failure. According to Sloan-Kettering hospital, only 20 percent of medical treatments proposed by physicians are based on trial-based evidence. One reason is because it would take a physician on average some 160 hours of reading to stay up to date on the latest literature. As if that were not enough, they would also have to decide what, if anything that they read had applicability to their patient's case. This is a task AI can perform in a matter of seconds after it has learned the specific domain. As proof of this, WellPoint, one of the largest healthcare companies in the nation, through their chief medical officer, stated that, "Watson's successful diagnosis rate for lung cancer is 90 percent, compared to 50 percent for human doctors."[13]

Deductive RCA, however, might be more difficult for machine learning at this stage, given that to get past the immediate and intermediate causes to the underlying cause, one has to ask "why" questions, which have elements of institutional and subjective knowledge (e.g., an employee's background and competency) that might not have been provided to the AI system. Fortunately, performing an RCA is not very complicated using existing techniques for business problems. AI would, however, be a highly beneficial assistant if conducting an RCA on a complex system or equipment that contains thousands of parts and components such as an airplane or space rocket.

The Potential of AI in Business

The fact that AI can access and sort through unstructured data (e.g., social media, including images and video, or call center customer service recordings going back a number of years), combined with its natural language interface, "democratizes" big data and its analysis, allowing any business person to pose questions, 24/7/365, and obtain answers in seconds. This will provide medium-sized and smaller companies with access to analytics expertise that was previously not available. For example, while most websites have some sort of web analytics package, such as Google Analytics, very few use it on a regular basis, or use it correctly. With AI, the web data monitoring and analysis could be performed by these AI systems and also generate easy-to-understand recommendations. In fact, if AI is integrated into the e-commerce platform, experiments can be conducted and changes automatically made to the content, layout or merchandise presentation so as to optimize the website.

Because AI is so new and will probably take many unexpected twists and turns as it moves forward, knowing which business areas will benefit the most is something of a work in progress. Moreover, given the secretive approach many of the key players are taking and the many issues being worked out, it will probably be several more years before AI becomes widely available or implementable by the average company. Watson's CTO explained that Watson's current deployment and learning time for a complex field like oncology is in the 12- to 18-month range because of the time needed to structure and feed in the data, teach AI the nomenclature and taxonomies in that discipline, and have it learn from the relevant clinical data; only then would it be in a position to start making sound recommendations. Can deep learning reduce this time frame? Maybe, but there will still be some setup and teaching when applying AI to a domain for the first time. Medicine is probably one of the more complicated and high-risk areas; after all, a wrong recommendation could result in injury or death. Faster implementations are possible in areas like finance, where Watson currently powers a self-service wealth advisor and customer service virtual agent at DBS Bank. Genesys, a leading provider of customer service agent assisted software, is also using Watson for smart customer service tools that learn and improve over time. These virtual assistant tools, whether web, email, or mobile app based, have the ability to learn, improve, and access a customer's data reaching back months and years to provide customized answers and recommendations in seconds. The Holy Grail of marketing, the much-hyped 1:1 personalization, may finally come to fruition with AI.

Figure E.2 shows some of the current areas and fields where AI is currently starting to be implemented and the likely impact it will have in certain areas of business in the near future. Any functional area where a significant amount of the work involves applying repetitive concepts and knowledge is at special risk (e.g., bookkeeping or logistics optimization type work). Those fields in which there are a variety of different problems and challenges, or where critical thinking and creativity play a major role, may at least during the first few iterations of AI be in a safer place than other professions. Unfortunately, as a percentage of jobs, those professions that rely on creativity and innovation are a very small percentage of the overall total.

We will also see disruption in many industries as robotics and AI pair up. For example, one relatively inexpensive robot (under $25,000 for the base model) called Baxter has the dexterity to perform many low-level repetitive human tasks found in shipping and logistic such as the handling of items, loading, packing and unpacking with the capacity to learn by observing others (e.g., a robot in a self-driving car delivering packages 24x7 is not that far-fetched).

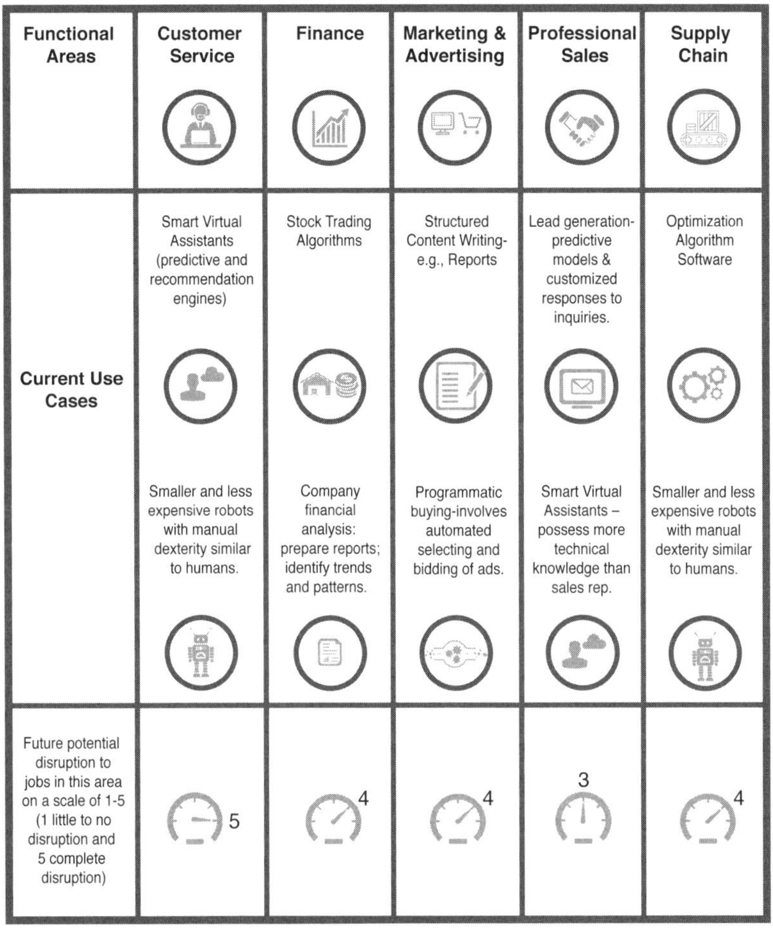

Figure E.2 Use cases of AI and disruption potential

Artificial Intelligence: The Known-Unknown

AI will undoubtedly play a growing role in many areas of business such as accounting, logistics, customer service, finance, marketing, and analytics. What we don't know is how soon, what its limitations will be, and what skills business professionals should retool for to survive this uncertain environment. This change probably won't happen within the next 5 or maybe 10 years, but it will probably start to have a significant impact 15 years from now. Related to this, and especially for those under the age of 30, is the question of what are the best careers and skills to pursue? For example, while today there is a shortage of qualified analytics professionals, as AI improves and learns more quickly, these professionals may need to refocus their efforts on machine learning algorithms, beginning with an understanding of the limitations of this technology, what is the best data to provide it, and how to effectively teach these systems and calibrate the results and ensure they make business sense. Human programming skills may become obsolete given how much better suited AI is to do that type of task and do so on a 24/7/365 basis, all while constantly improving its coding as each hour goes by.

The simplistic answer or solution for those less-technical professionals is to focus on those areas that AI and robotics cannot easily master, such as creativity, business innovation, and selling, or the execution and implementation of such ideas. Unfortunately, it is currently an unknown whether AI will remain incapable of innovation or creativity. We also know from the high failure rate of new businesses that innovation is not something most people are good at anyway. Moreover, large companies will be able to leverage AI and robotics and get into many business and industries that previously were unattractive because labor was a significant percentage of the cost structure, such as hospitality and labor-intensive areas of agriculture (e.g., vegetables or fruits) or construction. Another argument that could be made is that AI will augment instead of replace humans, which to some extent will happen, but this augmentation means increased productivity and inevitably the reduction or elimination of many supporting roles and jobs.

Our best hope is that robotics and AI will open up new markets and hence jobs in areas not easily scoped and foreseen by us presently, such as in accelerating the applicability and commercialization of nanotechnology, or ocean and space exploration and colonization.

Moreover if many jobs do in fact start to evaporate, the expectation and perhaps requirement from society should be that AI significantly reduce the cost of healthcare, food, clothing, energy, and housing so that people's reduced incomes have more buying power.

Finally, and as an educator, one interesting and challenging project so that we can deal in a more intelligent manner with this known-unknown future is to turn AI on its head. Rather than just *people* teaching the *machine,* perhaps AI could develop and personalize teaching plans customized to every individual's strengths and, at least to some extent, their weaknesses as well. With weaknesses, there should probably be some minimal baseline competency to be achieved; but if, for example, someone is not very quantitative yet has creative design skills, is there any point in wasting time on a skill that others are much better at? We see emerging use cases of this with programs such as CogMed that help children with disabilities improve certain cognitive functions using games that adjust to the user's level, skill, and improvements. However, what we are talking about is a much more in-depth and comprehensive approach focused on developing new skills and enhancing strengths over many years and across the board. Education should also consider and adapt to the fact that as AI becomes more prevalent, current techniques used in education such as extensive rote learning (memorization) may be both irrelevant and take time away from learning other skills.

The more relevant learning areas to leverage AI are in teaching people to:

- Learn better (and in the most relevant areas for that individual) and faster
- Be able to detect and prevent failure
- Engage a higher level of critical thinking and decision making than is normal
- Develop and enhance our creativity and innovation skills

If AI can be leveraged in this way and sooner rather than later, society will be better prepared to solve the employment and other challenges that AI will inevitably bring about. The jury is still out on the timing of, extent, and full impact of AI, but there can be little doubt that AI will be the most important domain transfer we may ever make; let's start off on the right foot.

Appendix

The Early Warning System-Details

In Chapter 4, page 78, we mentioned that additional details and examples for steps 5–9 would be provided in this section.

Step 5: Entering Leading, Lagging, and Connectors into a Spreadsheet

The sample spreadsheet, Table A.1, shows where the leading (columns A-D), connector (E–G), and lagging indicators (columns H-J) and variances are entered. You can also clearly see in the spreadsheet how after each forecasted indicator and connector assumption, that "actual" results or numbers from a campaign are entered.

Table A.1 covers in detail steps 5–9 from Chapter 4, "The Early Warning System," for creating the EWS.

Table A.1 Example of a Causal Forecast

Leading				Connector Assumptions			Lagging				
A	**B**	**C**	**D**	**E**	**F**	**G**	**H**	**I**	**J**	**K**	**L**
Promotional Drivers	**Forecast**	**Actual**	**Variance Formula: columns (C–B)/B**	**Conversion Rate (Forecasted)**	**Conversion Rate (Actual)**	**Variance conversion Rate Formula: columns (F–E)/E**	**New Customer Orders (Forecasted)**	**New Customer Orders (Actual)**	**Variance New Customer Orders Formula: columns I–H**	**Weights Based on Forecast**	**EWS Weighed Variance**
Organic web traffic (e.g., YouTube, Twitter, SEO): unique visitors	50,000	46,000	–8%	0.20%	0.17%	–15%	100	78	(22)	0.30	(6.6)
Web traffic from affiliates: unique visitors	5,000	5,300	6%	0.015%	0.018%	20%	1	1	0	0.00	0
PPC-visible impressions based on average 1.5 ad rank	5,000	5,300	6%	2.50%	1.80%	–28%	125	95	(30)	0.38	(11.1)

	Leading			Connector Assumptions			Lagging				
A	B	C	D	E	F	G	H	I	J	K	L
Promotional Drivers	**Forecast**	**Actual**	**Variance Formula: columns (C–B)/B**	**Conversion Rate (Forecasted)**	**Conversion Rate (Actual)**	**Variance conversion Rate Formula: columns (F–E)/E**	**New Customer Orders (Forecasted)**	**New Customer Orders (Actual)**	**Variance New Customer Orders Formula: columns I–H**	**Weights Based on Forecast**	**EWS Weighed Variance**
Number of on-hold messages with partner companies	640	450	–30%	0.48%	0.35%	–27%	3	2	(1)	0.01	(0.01)
Number of mail-order catalogs mailed	300	280	–7%	3.0%	3.2%	7%	9	9	(0)	0.03	(0)
Number of people attending PR events	1,500	1,600	7%	3.0%	2.2%	–27%	45	35	(10)	0.14	(1.3)
Number of fliers mailed	2,000	1,800	–10%	2.5%	1.0%	–60%	50	18	(32)	0.15	(4.8)
Totals							333	238	(95)		(24)

Step 6: Calculating the Variance

The "actual" results are the numbers that come in after you obtained results from the different initiatives (column A). Once actuals are entered, the variance can be calculated as shown in columns D, G, and J.

Most variance calculations are pretty straightforward (e.g., [Actual results-Forecasted results]/Forecasted results). However, as the excerpt in Table A.2 shows, some leading indicators are about maintaining a certain market share level, position, or ranking and thus a lower number is better (e.g., an average PPC ad rank position of 1.5 is better than a position of 3, so going from 1.5 to a 3 is actually a decrease or negative). Therefore in these cases, add a negative number if and when the higher position, rank, or share decreases, as shown in the Table A.2. In the case of rankings, beause the scale is often non-linear (e.g., a ranking drop from ad rank position 1 to 2 may have a greater negative impact than a drop from ad rank 2 to position 3) you might want to create an additional weighed variance.

Table A.2 Example of an Assumption Where a Lower Number (Ranking) Is Better and Negative Variance Is Shown When You Drop Position

Assumptions	Forecast	Actual	Variance
Average ad rank position PPC	1.5	2.2	–47%

Step 7: Calculating a Weighed Scored

This step requires calculating weights so that you can prioritize your warning system by what has the most impact. In this model, it is calculated as a percentage of the total forecasted number of orders as shown in Table A.1, column K. Once the weights have been calculated, multiply columns J by K to get the EWS score, as shown in column L.

Each driver should have its own individually weighted score, which can be negative or positive, with a cumulative score for all the lagging indicators. In this example, the overall EWS score is a –24, with the underperformance from the organic web traffic and PPC initiatives having had the biggest "drag effect" on the overall performance.

Insight

We did not assign any weights to the leading indicators because they often have different types of measurements (e.g., impressions, unique visitors, on-hold messages, referrals, mailed pieces). As a result, assigning weights with leading indicators can be problematic and as a result are usually not an apple to apples comparison.

Step 8: The Early Warning System Dashboard

Table A.3 shows what the EWS section of your business dashboard might look like. These measures are all entirely customizable, with some companies perhaps wanting to show only negative variances to reduce the clutter.

Table A.3 Early Warning System Dashboard

Early Warning System	Variance
Assumptions	
Average ad rank position PPC	–47%
Organic search page average rank for top five converting keywords	–60%
Awareness index (= Positive Mentions / Total Category Mentions)	233%
Distribution (= # Outlets In / Total # Of Outlets)	–29%
Number of complaints per week	25%

Promotional Leading Drivers	Variance Leading Indicators	Variance Conversion rate	Variance New Customer Orders	EWS Weighed Variance Score
Organic web traffic (from blog, YouTube, Twitter, Instagram and SEO): unique visitors	–8%	–15%	–22	**–6.6**
Web traffic from affiliates: unique visitors	6%	20%	0	**0.00**
PPC-visible impressions	6%	–28%	–30	**–11.12**
Number of on-hold messages with partner companies	–30%	–27%	–1	**–0.01**
Number of mail-order catalogs mailed	–7%	7%	0	**0.00**
Number of people attending PR events	7%	–27%	–10	**–1.33**
Number of fliers mailed	–10%	–60%	–32	**–4.8**
Totals			**–95**	**–24**

Step 9: Troubleshooting: When the EWS Shows Underperformance

A key benefit of the EWS is that when failure or underperformance occurs, much of the investigative work will have been done for you. While many of the causes uncovered by the EWS will allow you to take quick corrective action, these will usually be the immediate or proximate causes of failure or underperformance and therefore not the root causes.

Once a negative score or variance appears, determine (e.g., Table A.4) whether the problem resides with a leading indicator (e.g., a decrease in the number of unique visitors) or with the "connector" assumption (e.g., a lower-than-expected conversion rate). If something is very straightforward, the troubleshooting can end there (e.g., reallocate your promotional budget to better-performing drivers or adjust your assumptions or connector variables). However, if it involves several factors and possible causes, it is best to conduct a *root cause analysis* (RCA). As argued in Chapter 3, "The Business Failure Audit and the Domain Transfer of Root Cause Analysis," businesses need to stop focusing on immediate causes if they want more permanent solutions to their problems.

When multiple negative variances appear, focus on the higher EWS scores because those are the ones that will impact the lagging indicators (e.g., revenue) the most. In Table A.4, we are only highlighting two important negative indicators. Without running a regression, there is probably some correlation between some of the assumptions and the negative outcomes. For example, the loss in "average ad rank position" is probably a contributor to the negative leading indicator "PPC" and its poor conversion rate. When an ad rank drops (becomes less visible to most prospects), you can assume based on experience and historical data that the click-through rate and conversion rate will also decrease.

Table A.4 Negative Variances for Troubleshooting

Promotional Leading Drivers	Variance Leading Indicators	Variance Conversion Rate	Variance New Customer Orders	EWS Weighed Variance
PPC-visible impressions based on average 1.5 ad rank	6%	–28%	–30	–11.12
Number of fliers mailed	–10%	–60%	–32	–4.81

Digging Deeper

Before proceeding on to an RCA, always start by looking at the assumptions section and the evidence upon which these assumptions were made. This is often where the issue lies. In the example of the fliers that were mailed and the incorrect average conversion rate assumption, it might be because the assumption was based on a previous flier that had an attractive incentive, whereas the new underperforming flier did not have any incentive, and therefore an inappropriate benchmark was used as an assumption.

Now that you know how an RCA works, you can follow the example in Table A.5. The key when performing the RCA is to eliminate those causes you listed that did not contribute to the underperformance (crossed out in Table A.5) and then ask "why" questions with the remaining causes until you arrive at the root cause.

Table A.5 Root Cause Analysis of an EWS Variance

	Leading			Connector Assumptions		
A	B	C	D	E	F	G
Promotional Drivers	Forecast	Actual	Variance	Conversion Rate (Forecasted)	Conversion Rate (Actual)	Variance Conversion Rate
# of Fliers Mailed	2,000	1,800	-10%	2.5%	1.0%	-60%

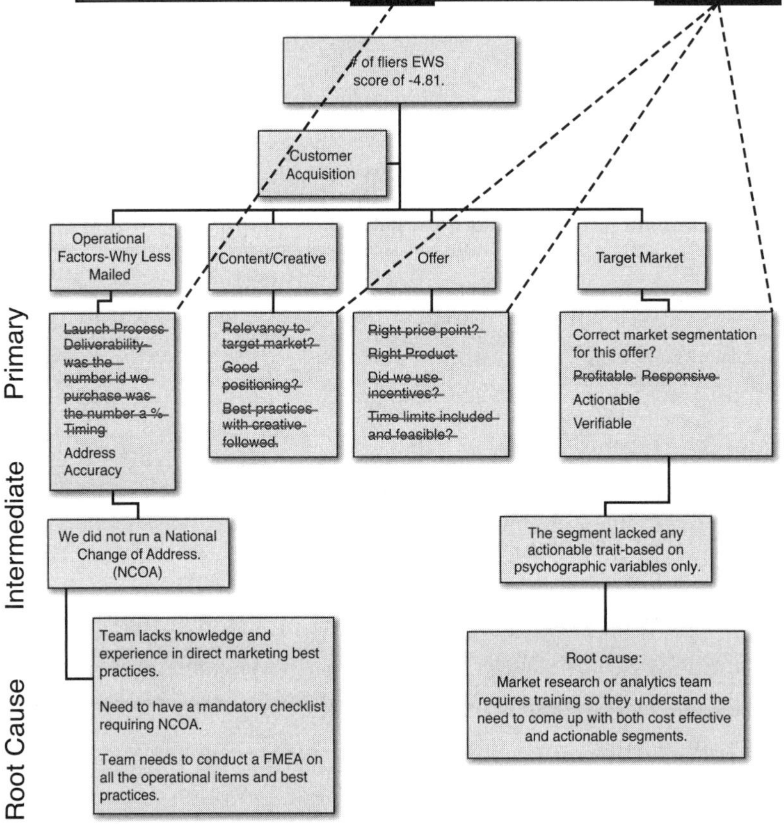

The Return on Promotion (ROP)

In Chapter 5, mention was made of a simple and quick forecast that can be used for any promotional activity that has a cost associated with it. The Return on Promotion is a tool that can help you decide, *a priori,* if you should spend money on a public relations event, the hiring of a sales representative, running an ad, undertaking a direct mail, email, PPC, or any other type of promotional effort. The ROP consists of an estimate of all the costs that are specific to the initiative being planned.

Section A, shows how many postcards you plan to send out, the assumed conversion rate, and the estimated number of orders you expect to get based on your experience or benchmark.

Section A	
Name of piece	Customer acquisition, 4 color, both sides, 6 × 9 postcard
Number of postcards to be mailed	50,000
Conversion rate	2%
Forecast number of orders generated	1,000

Section B is where you include a detailed breakdown of all the costs that this promotional or sales effort entails.

Section B	
Cost for This Promotion	**Total Cost**
Copy writing and revisions	$650
Graphic design	$600
Proofs	$200
Printing	
Postcard	$4,979
Lists	
List rental	$12,500
Lettershop	
Inserting	$1,500
Sorting, mailing	$300

Section B (continued)	
Postage	
Postage out	$13,500
Telemarketing	
Setting up 800 number	$500
Inbound	$1,000
Misc.	$650
Totals	**$36,379**

Section C is a detailed breakdown of not just your sales price and product costs, but also of all the other expenses that the proposed initiative will generate such as returns, packaging materials, shipping costs, and so on. In this section you also determine your "allowable," which is roughly your gross profit (minus some additional expenses detailed in this section).

Section C		
Breakeven Analysis	**Subtotals**	**Totals**
Average order		
Purchase or manufacturing cost	28	
Freight	2	
Subtotal		$30.00
Order processing		
O/E purchasing, etc.	1.1	
Packing materials	0.4	
Misc.	0.8	
Subtotal		$2.30
Billing and collections		
Credit card processing charges (.03)	0.84	
Returns (app. .25% return)	0.123	
Subtotal		$0.96
Cost per order		**$33.26**
Average selling price		$59.99
Less cost per order		$33.26
ALLOWABLE		**$26.73**

The essence and value of the ROP resides in section D. With the allowable figure in hand, you can estimate how many orders you actually need to sell to reach a breakeven point, what conversion rate is needed, and, based on the estimated number of orders, what revenue and net profit this initiative would generate. In the last calculation, your promotional costs (section B) are subtracted from your net profit.

Section D	
Return on Promotion	
Number of orders needed to break even (promotional costs/allowable)	**1,361**
Conversion rate needed to break even (breakeven orders/number of fliers mailed)	**2.72%**
Forecasted revenue (Number of orders forecasted * Average selling price)	$59,990
Forecasted net profit (Revenue –Costs)	$26,727
Forecasted net profit after promotional costs (Forecasted net profit –total promotional costs)	–$9,652
Forecasted return on promotion (Net profit on promotion/Total promotional costs)	–27%

With this information, you can now make a more intelligent and informed choice. Based on the needed breakeven conversion rate and negative ROP in this example, you should go back and see if you can reduce your costs, or change the type of initiative (because increasing the price is usually not an option), or even scrap the proposed initiative all together. As discussed in Chapter 2, "Don't Start Off on the Wrong Foot," one thing that should be done before jumping in is to analyze as many options as possible, remembering that sometimes and for the time being, the best choice might be to do nothing.

Endnotes

Chapter 1, "Failure & Stagnation"

1. Griffin and Paul Belliveau, Drivers of NPD Success. The 1997 PDMA Report (Chicago, Product Development & Management Association, 1997).
2. D.S. Hopkins, New Product Winners and Losers, Conference Board Report #773, 1980.
3. Booz Allen Hamilton, *New Product Management for the 1980s* (New York; Booz Allen Hamilton).
4. Bill Gorman, New Product News, 1990.
5. Christopher Powers, "Flops," *Business Week,* August 16, 1993, Number 3332, 76.
6. Linton, Matysiak, and Wilkes, Marketing, Witchcraft or Science, 1997.
7. Robert G. Cooper, *Winning at New Products,* 2nd Edition, 1993, 8.
8. Christopher Powers, "Flops," *Business Week,* August 16, 1993, Number 3332, 76.
9. Booz Allen Hamilton, *New Product Management for the 1980s* (New York; Booz Allen Hamilton).
10. "P&G Closes On-Line Cosmetics Business," by Cosmetics Design, June 14, 2005.

11. "H.P., Tech Powerhouse, Stumbles in Smartphones," *New York Times*, February 24, 2010.
12. Alvin Achenbaum, "How to Succeed in New Products," *Advertising Age*, June 26, 1989, 62.
13. K. Clancy and P. Krieg, *Your Gut Is Still Not Smarter Than Your Head* (Wiley, 2007), 14.
14. The Breakthrough Innovation Report, 2014, by The Nielsen Company.
15. National Federation of Independent Business Education Foundation, 1997.
16. D.S. Hopkins, New Product Winners and Losers, Conference Board Report #773, 1980.
17. R. Hill and J. Hlavacek, "Learning from Failure, Ten Guidelines for Venture Management," *California Management Review*, Summer Volume XIX No. 4, 1977.
18. K. Clancy and R. Shulman, *The Marketing Revolution*, 2nd edition (Harper Perennial, 1993), 8–9.
19. Idem, 207.
20. John Mullins and R. Komisar, "Getting to Plan B: Breaking Through to a Better Business Model," *Harvard Business Review Press*, 2009.

Chapter 2, "Don't Start Off on the Wrong Foot"

1. Rolf Dobelli, *The Art of Thinking Clearly* (New York: Harper Collins Publisher, 2014), 129.
2. Daniel Kahneman, *Think Fast Think Slow* (New York: Farrar, Straus and Giroux, 2010), 20–21.

3. J. Edward Russo and Paul Schoemaker, *Decision Traps* (Chicago: Product Development & Management Association, 1997), 37.

4. "Ford Pinto," Engineering.com, October 24, 2006.

5. Michael A. Anleitner, *The Power of Deduction: Failure Mode and Effects Analysis* (Milwaukee, WI: ASQ Quality Press, 2010), 5.

6. Bryce Hoffman, "Bad Blood Cited Between GM, Ignition Switch Supplier Delphi," Detriotnews.com, April 14, 2014.

7. Junko Ogura, "Takata Accused of Putting Profits Ahead of Safety," CNNMoney, June 22, 2015. Accessed June 27, 2015.

8. Atul Gawande, *The Checklist Manifesto* (New York: Metropolitan Books, 2009), 44–45.

9. Idem.

Chapter 3, "The Business Failure Audit and the Domain Transfer of Root Cause Analysis"

1. Paul Gompers, Anna Kovner, Josh Lerner, and David Scharfstein, "Performance Persistence in Entrepreneurship," *Journal of Financial Economics* 96 (2010): 18–32.

2. "NASA Root Cause Analysis Supplemental Training Manual," by Faith Chandler, Director of Mishap Investigation and Human Reliability, Office of the Chief Technologist, NASA Headquarters, Washington DC, 2008.

3. Alexander Edsel, "The Blame Game: When Launches Fail, Try a Product Failure Audit to Identify the Cause or Causes," *PDMA Visions Magazine*, March 2011.

Chapter 4, "The Early Warning System"

1. "The Altman Z-Score: Is It Possible to Predict Corporate Bankruptcy Using a Formula?" *Business Insider,* April 13, 2011. Accessed June 18, 2015.
2. Edward Altman, "Financial Ratios, Discriminant Analysis and the Prediction of Corporate Bankruptcy," *The Journal of Finance,* Volume 23, Issue 4, September 1, 1968. Accessed June 25, 2015.
3. "Leading Economic Index (LEI) for the U.S. Increased Again," The Conference Board. Accessed June 18, 2015.

Chapter 5, "Blind Spots and Traps"

1. Žižek, Slavoj, "Philosophy, the 'Unknown Knowns,' and the Public Use of Reason," *Topoi* 25, no. 1 (2006), 137–42.
2. Peter Tuckel, Elaine Leppo, and Barbara Kaplan, "Focus Groups Under Scrutiny. Why People Go and How It Affects Their Attitudes Toward Participation," *Marketing Research* Vol. 4, Issue 2 (June 1992). Accessed November 9, 2014.
3. John P. A. Ioannidis, "Why Most Published Research Findings Are False (Essay)," *PLoS Medicine* 2, no. 8 (2005): E12.
4. "Scientific Papers Often Overstate Findings, Texas A&M Statistician Finds," Texas A&M Science. Accessed June 20, 2015.
5. Nina Bai, "Do That Again," *The Scientist,* August 15, 2012. Accessed January 5, 2015.
6. Mitchell Martin, "Iridium Fails to Find a Market: Satellite Phone Misses Its Orbit," *New York Times,* October 8, 1999. Accessed December 12, 2014.
7. Susan Fournier, "Introducing New Coke," HBR Case Study 9-5000-067, October 31, 2001.

8. Mark Holtzman, Mark, Elizabeth Venuti, and Robert Fonfeder. "Enron and the Raptors," April 3, 2003. Accessed January 6, 2015.
9. Kevin Clancy and R. Shulman, *The Marketing Revolution,* 2nd edition, (Harper Perennial, 1993): 91.
10. "Black Friday Report 2012," IBM Digital Analytics Benchmark Black Friday Report 2012.
11. "Americans Say Social Media Have Little Sway on Purchases," Accessed June 19, 2015.
12. R. Culpepper and R. A. Zimmermann, "Culture-Based Extreme Response Bias in Surveys Employing Variable Response Items: An Investigation of Response Tendency Among Hispanic-Americans," *Journal of International Business Research,* (Fall 2006): 75-83
13. John T. Gourville and Christina L. Darwall, "Microsoft: Launching the Smart Watch," Harvard Business School Case 504-004, October 2003. (Revised January 2005): 9–10.
14. Ben Goldacre, "Trial Sans Error: How Pharma-Funded Research Cherry-Picks Positive Results [Excerpt]," *Scientific American,* February 13, 2013. Accessed January 6, 2015.
15. Katie Thomas, "In Documents on Pain Drug, Signs of Doubt and Deception," *New York Times,* June 24, 2012. Accessed January 6, 2015.
16. Stephen Few, "Visual Perception and Quantitative Communication," In *Show Me the Numbers: Designing Tables and Graphs to Enlighten*, 2004 ed. (Oakland, Calif.: Analytics Press, 2004), 92–95.
17. Roni Caryn Rabin, "New Concerns on Robotic Surgeries," *New York Times,* September 9, 2013.
18. James T.Breeden, MD, "Statement on Robotic Surgery," Acog.org. March 14, 2013.

19. Stephen P. Luby et al. "The "Effect of Handwashing on Child Health: A Randomized Controlled Trial," *Lancet* Vol. 366 (July 16, 2005).

20. Sarah Butler, "Fresh, But Not So Easy: Tesco Joins a Long List of British Failures in America," *Guardian*, December 8, 2012.

21. Roger Lowenstein, "Long-Term Capital Management: It's a Short-Term Memory," *New York Times,* September 7, 2008. Accessed January 6, 2015.

22. Nate Silver, *The Signal and the Noise: Why Most Predictions Fail—but Some Don't* (New York: Penguin Press, 2012), 45.

23. "Fourth Quarter 2007 Survey of Professional Forecasters," Federal Reserve Bank of Philadelphia, November 3, 2007. Accessed January 6, 2015.

24. Philip E. Tetlock and Ebrary, Inc. *Expert Political Judgment How Good Is It? How Can We Know?* (Princeton, N.J.: Princeton University Press, 2005).

25. P. Cross, "Not Can but Will College Teachers Be Improved?" *New Directions for Higher Education* 17 (1977): 1–15.

26. "The Bayesian Approach to Forecasting," Oracle Whitepaper, September 1, 2006. Accessed January 6, 2015.

27. Andy Bauer et al. "Forecast Evaluation with Cross-Sectional Data: The Blue Chip Surveys," *The Free Library*, April 1, 2003. Accessed January 5, 2015.

28. Clayton M. Christensen, *The Innovator's Dilemma: When New Technologies Cause Great Firms to Fail* (Boston: Harvard Business School Press, 1997).

Chapter 6, "The Preplanned Exit Strategy"

1. Julie Creswell and Vikas Bajaj, "$3.2 Billion Move by Bear Stearns to Rescue Fund," *New York Times,* June 22, 2007. Accessed June 18, 2015.
2. Geoffrey Moore, *Crossing the Chasm* (Harper Business Book, 1999), 77.
3. "The Kleenex Brand Story," Kleenex.com. Accessed June 18, 2015.
4. Philip Kotler, "Harvesting Strategies for Weak Products," *Business Horizons,* 15–22.
5. "Autos," *Los Angeles Times,* December 5, 1992. Accessed June 30, 2015.
6. Van V. Miller and John Quinn, "The Harvest Strategy: How to Implement a Disaster for the Environment and the Stockholders," *Business Strategy and the Environment* (1998): 71–89.

Epilogue

1. "2014 Statistics," *The Bar Examiner* 84(1), Accessed May 18, 2015
2. "2014 Examination Results," The American Board of Family Medicine. Accessed May 18, 2015
3. "Uniform CPA Passing Rates 2014," The American Institute of CPAs.
4. "Computer Simulating 13-Year-Old Boy Becomes First to Pass Turing Test," *Guardian,* June 9, 2014. Accessed June 29, 2015.
5. "IBM Watson: The Inside Story of How the Jeopardy-Winning Supercomputer Was Born, and What It Wants to Do Next," *TechRepublic.* Accessed June 18, 2015.

6. Tom Simonite, "Thinking in Silicon," *MIT Technology Review*. Accessed June 18, 2015.
7. Marcus Woo and Cade Metz, "Google's AI Is Now Smart Enough to Play Atari Like the Pros," Wired.com, February 25, 2015. Accessed June 29, 2015.
8. "The Next Big Thing You Missed: The Quest to Give Computers the Power of Imagination," Wired.com, Conde Nast Digital. Accessed June 18, 2015.
9. Yuki Kono et al. "Frontal Face Generation from Multiple Low-Resolution Non-Frontal Faces for Face Recognition," Computer Vision – ACCV 2010 Workshops Lecture Notes in Computer Science, 2015, 175–83.
10. Antonio Regalado, "Is Google Cornering the Market on Deep Learning?" *MIT Technology Review*, January 29, 2014. Accessed June 29, 2015.
11. "IBM Watson Ecosystem," Accessed June 29, 2015.
12. "AI Found Better Than Doctors at Diagnosing, Treating Patients." Computerworld. Accessed June 18, 2015.
13. "IBM's Watson Is Better at Diagnosing Cancer Than Human Doctors." Wired UK. Accessed June 18, 2015.

Index

F

N

O

P

Q-R

S

T

U

V

W

X-Y-Z